£7.99

CHELSEA END 50-YEAR WAIT TO LAND THE TITLE
BLUE
IS THE COLOUR!

Chelsea's fans are looking for Mour after The Blues won their first championship for 50 years. Two league titles, the Portuguese Cup, UEFA Cup and the Champions League in just two seasons at Porto was an impressive CV, but little did people know just how big Jose Mourinho's impact would be when he walked into Stamford Bridge for the first time on July 5, 2004.

He spent £90m before the season kicked off and many pundits said that he wouldn't be able to win the Premiership in his first year because he had too many new players to blood into the side.

But he proved them all wrong as Chelsea blasted their way to the title with 12 points to spare and lifted the Carling Cup. Skipper John Terry admits: "When Mr Mourinho first came it was a chance for the new players and also the ones from last season to impress. For me, the new manager coming in was certainly a motivation. I'd die for the man, both on and off the pitch.

"He gave me a real boost early on saying that I was going to be captain which meant everything to me. He has been inspirational. He is one of the lads really, he's really relaxed in training and all the lads have a great respect for who he is and what he is trying to achieve. We all love him."

Keeper Petr Cech, who kept a record ten consecutive clean sheets during the season is also a Mourinho fan.

"He came to England, which presented a new culture a new style of football, and brought in new players and won two trophies," said Petr. "We created a new team with a new manager and it is always difficult to play well in the first season together. To do so well was fantastic."

The Czech Republic star has warned the other 19 sides in the top-flight: "We have a great team and the club is ready for the title again. Of course it is going to be difficult, because to win the Premiership two seasons running is always difficult. Our expectations were high last season and they are going to be even higher now."

THE BLUE FACTS FROM 2004-05

- Chelsea never lost a game by more than one goal, and set a new Premiership best with just 15 goals conceded.
- Their top scorer was midfielder Frank Lampard (19).
- They set a new record with 28 Premiership wins.
- The Blues' 95 points were the most ever earned in the Premiership.
- John Terry was named PFA Player of the Season, the first defender to win the title in 12 years. Frank Lampard won the Football Writers' award.
- Petr Cech and Arjen Robben were named along with Lampard and Terry in the Premiership team of the season, picked by their fellow professionals.
- They were the only side not to have a player sent off during the Premiership campaign.

LIVERPOOL THE KINGS OF EUROPE

A NIGHT TO REMEMBER...

WHEN THEY were 3-0 down before half-time no one gave Liverpool a chance in their Champions League Final against AC Milan. But they brought the scores level, survived extra-time and then won a dramatic penalty shoot-out to lift their fifth European Cup.

COMPLIMENTS OF THE SEASON

The teams and players who ended season 2004-05 as winners!

SUNDERLAND

CHAMPIONSHIP CHAMPIONS

Mick McCarthy guided Sunderland to the Premiership despite lowering the wage bill and spending very little. The Black Cats held off the challenges of Wigan and Ipswich and stormed to the Championship after a late end-of-season surge. Their star performers were 16-goal Marcus Stewart, Argentine left-sided defender-midfielder Julio Arca, arguably one of the best performers outside of the top-flight, and defender Steve Caldwell who signed for nothing from local rivals Newcastle. They were joined in the automatic promotion places by Wigan. West Ham won the play-off final against Preston 1-0.

LUTON TOWN
LEAGUE ONE CHAMPIONS

The Hatters made it into the Championship an impressive 12 points ahead of second-placed Hull City. Mike Newell's first full season as boss was helped by the goal-scoring exploits of striker Steve Howard and midfielders Ahmet Brkovic and Kevin Nicholls. Hull, managed by England Under-21 boss Peter Taylor clinched the second automatic promotion spot thanks to the return of local hero Nicky Barmby. Sheffield Wednesday also earned a Championship place after beating Hartlepool 4-2 in the play-off final.

BARNET
CONFERENCE CHAMPIONS

After four seasons in the Conference, Barnet regained their League status 12 points ahead of nearest challengers Hereford. Their boss Paul Fairclough, also manager of England's National team for non-League players, built a young squad with hints of experience, including 29-goal top scorer Guliano Grazioli. Carlisle bounced back through the play-offs at the first attempt when they beat Stevenage 1-0.

YEOVIL TOWN
LEAGUE TWO CHAMPIONS

Gary Johnson's managerial reputation was enhanced further as the former Latvia boss guided The Glovers to their highest-ever League standing. Former Everton striker Phil Jevons was impressive, banging in 27 league goals.

RANGERS
SCOTTISH PREMIER LEAGUE & CIS CUP

Celtic lost 2-1 to Motherwell on the final day of the season, thanks to two goals from Bhoys' fan Scott McDonald and that allowed Rangers to snatch the title from their Glasgow rivals. Ironically, Rangers had thumped Motherwell 5-1 to claim the Scottish League Cup for the 24th time, with Greek defender Sotirios Kyrgiakos scoring a double.

CELTIC
SCOTTISH CUP

Martin O'Neill collected his seventh trophy with Celtic just days after announcing he was quitting Parkhead. Alan Thompson scored from a deflected free-kick against Dundee United after just 11 minutes.

ARSENAL
FA CUP

A crunch game between two sides desperately needing silverware saw Man United very much in control, but after goal-less normal and extra-time the first-ever FA Cup Final penalty shoot-out saw The Gunners win 5-4, skipper Patrick Vieira scoring the decisive spot-kick. Often-criticised German keeper Jens Lehmann was their hero with a series of saves, including one from the spot by Paul Scholes.

CHELSEA
CARLING CUP

Jose Mourinho claimed his first trophy in English football after an exciting and controversial encounter against Liverpool in Cardiff. Liverpool took the lead after just 45 seconds, but Chelsea equalised with around ten minutes to go through a Steven Gerrard own goal. The equaliser saw Mourinho put his fingers to his lips apparently hushing the Liverpool fans. Extra-time goals from Didier Drogba and Mateja Kezman gave The Blues a 3-2 victory.

WREXHAM
LDV VANS TROPHY

The cash-strapped Welsh side were triumphant in Cardiff after a closely fought contest with Southend United. Juan Ugarte and Darren Ferguson, son of Sir Alex, gave Wrexham a 2-0 extra time victory.

GRAYS ATHLETIC
FA TROPHY

Former England Schoolboys keeper Ashley Bayes saved two spot-kicks as Grays Athletic beat Hucknall to win non-League's biggest piece of silverware. The teams were 1-1 after extra-time at Villa Park, and Grays took the penalty shoot-out 6-5.

DIDCOT TOWN
FA VASE

Stuart Beavon scored twice at White Hart Lane – a ground where his father played – as Didcot beat AFC Sudbury 3-2. The Suffolk side became beaten finalists for the third successive season.

CSKA MOSCOW
UEFA CUP

CSKA Moscow, the team supported by £29m from Chelsea owner Roman Abramovich's oil company, won the UEFA Cup 3-1, despite playing the final at the home of their opponents, Portugal's Sporting Lisbon. It was the first European trophy won by a Russian side.

JOHN TERRY
PFA PLAYER OF THE YEAR

Chelsea's captain was a man mountain, holding The Blues' impressive defence together and contributing some vital goals, particularly in Europe. His team-mate Frank Lampard walked off with the Football Writers' Footballer of the Year award.

WAYNE ROONEY
PFA YOUNG PLAYER OF THE YEAR

After an impressive Euro 2004 for England, Wayne made a £27m move from Everton to Manchester United. He announced his arrival at Old Trafford with a cracking debut hat-trick against Fenerbahce in the Champions League and went on to score some crucial, spectacular and truly memorable goals throughout the season.

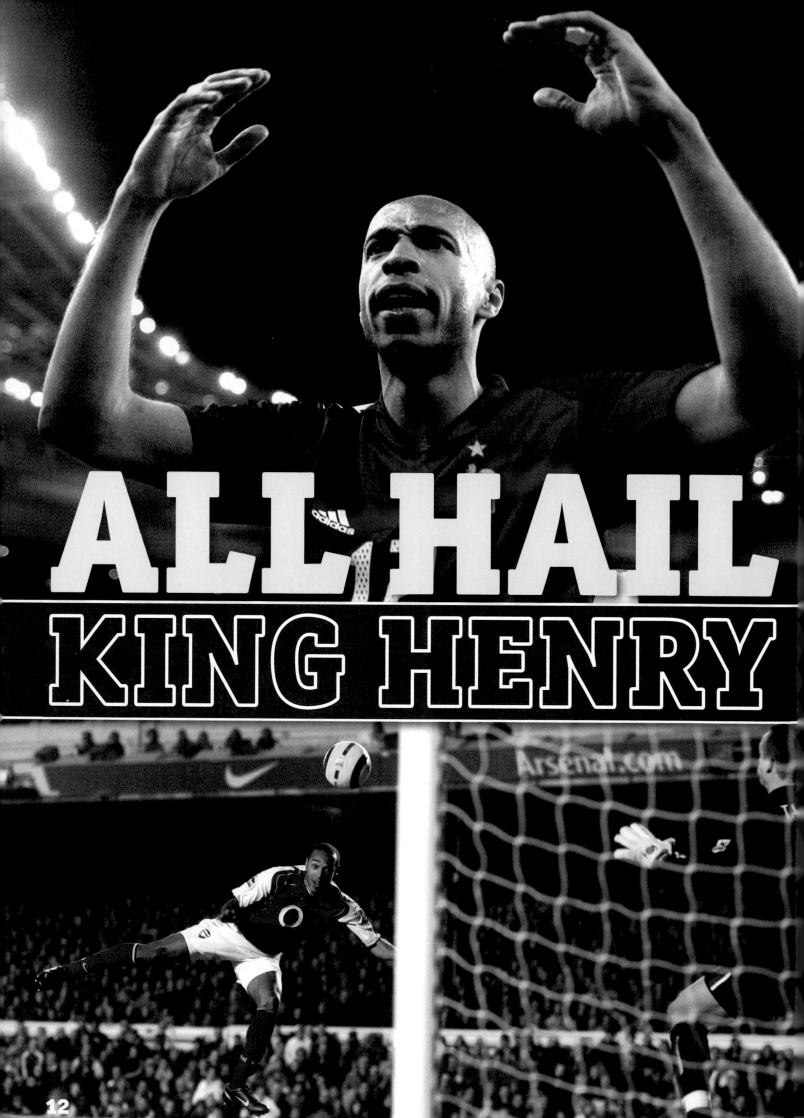

ALL HAIL
KING HENRY

Dennis Bergkamp
– Arsenal striker

"He's reached 100 goals in three-and-a-half years – that's an amazing record. I think Thierry's got everything a striker needs. He has so much pace, skill and strength. With his speed there's not a defender in the world who will be able to stop him."

Alan Shearer
– Newcastle skipper

"People say he doesn't score a lot of goals with his head, but does he really have to with the ability he has in his feet? He makes spectacular goals look easy. His technique is fantastic."

Ruud Van Nistelrooy
–Man United striker

"With his pace and vision, his scoring ability and his ability to gel with others – it would be fantastic to play with him. To see his game and my game as a duo would be fantastic."

Arsene Wenger
– Arsenal boss

"He's made the difference for us in many big games. When we expect him to do it, he does it. He's an exceptional world-class player. His physical performances have been absolutely outstanding. Aside from his talent, the effort he puts in is so impressive."

Sven Goran Eriksson
– England boss

"Henry has got so much pace it is frightening, he really is incredible – he could sell pace he has so much! He also scores goals and if you give him half a yard he's gone and you will be in trouble. He first really made an impression when he came to Arsenal but I knew of him when he was at Juventus. Looking back it is amazing that they sold him. "

Marcel Desailly
– ex-France captain

"Thierry came into the national team in 1998 for the World Cup. He was 19 years-old and he was already quick, but he has improved a lot since then. He has improved because he is an intelligent player. He is really clever in his lifestyle and also on the pitch. He has also been humble and has listened to what people around him are saying, especially Arsene Wenger."

Patrick Vieira
– former Arsenal captain

"Thierry is, by far, the best striker in world football. He doesn't just score goals, there is a lot more to his game than that. Even when he's not having a good day he can make an important pass. He is a strong character. If things go wrong, he bounces straight back. His effect on the club is very big."

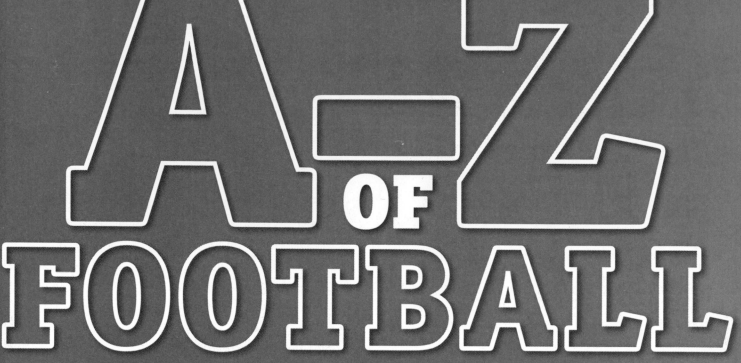

A-Z OF FOOTBALL

A whistle-stop tour of the wonderful world of professional football

A — Argentina
Forget Brazil, Holland and even the Germans, this is the side England – and David Beckham – really like to beat the most.

C — Chelsea
Bankrolled by Abramovich's millions, the current Premier League champions look like becoming the biggest force in football. But don't tell Fergie!

B — Bosman
The transfer ruling – named after Belgian footballer Jean-Marc Bosman – that allows players to leave at the end of their contract on a "free." Clubs are powerless, players call the shots and agents are laughing all the way to the bank.

D — David Beckham
Mr Posh, fashion idol, celebrity icon – and he can play football a bit too – the England captain is one of the most well-known faces on the planet. Think Victoria is a wee bit jealous?

E Europe

Although the Premiership is the "bread and butter," success in the Champions League represents the true gauge of a team's greatness.

F Fans

Despite the multi-millions earned by the stars, the game still belongs to us!

G Goals

Yes, we like the tackling and we appreciate the value of a strong defence but who wants to see boring 0-0s? Football is about goals and lots of them.

H Hurst

Sir Geoff scored a hat-trick in the World Cup Final of 1966 and led England to victory. Forty years on, can Michael Owen do the same?

I Imports

Cantona, Zola, Bergkamp, Henry, Vieira, Van Nistelrooy... the list goes on. Where would the Premiership be without our brilliant foreigners?

J John Terry

Chelsea's captain and inspiration, voted PFA Player of the Year. Expect him to lead England before too long.

K Knee

The worst kind of injury to befall any player. A dreaded "cruciate" and your career can be over before it has really started.

L Lineker

Former England captain and goalscorer supreme, Gary Lineker played for Leicester City, Everton, Barca and Tottenham. He's now the face of BBC One's legendary *Match of the Day*.

Metatarsal

The most fashionable injury of recent times as David Beckham and Gary Neville can testify. Fancy name but to you and me it means "broken foot."

Ninety-Six

As in Euro '96. Still ranks as the most magical, and painful tournament that most can remember! Gareth Southgate's penalty miss in the semi-final against West Germany was a moment of high drama.

Opinions

Football is a game of opinions, or so they say, and we all think we know better than the manager. In Jacques Santini's case we were probably right!

Penalties

The cruellest way to go out of any competition, although England do tend to make a habit out of it. Heroes and villains are made in an instant.

Quit

The other way of saying "the fans hate me, the players laugh when I give a team talk and the chairman thinks I'm an idiot, I better jump before I am pushed."

Ronaldinho

The most exciting talent on the planet and the current FIFA World Player of the Year. Nice skills, shame about the teeth...

Sir Alex

The most influential and successful manager in Premiership history. But woe betide anyone who gets on his wrong side! Just ask Lee Sharpe, Jaap Stam, Mark Bosnich, Dwight Yorke...

Tapping Up

Otherwise known as making an illegal approach to a player (or manager) who is under contract to another club. A speciality of the Chelsea regime.

U United

As in Man United. The dominant team of the 1990s and even some of the Noughties – no wonder Malcolm Glazer wanted them so badly.

V Value for Money

Is 30 quid for an hour and a half's entertainment really a sound investment? Hundreds of thousands of football fans seem to think so every Saturday.

W World Cup

The pinnacle of any international team's aspirations. Brazil are the most successful team ever in this competition although the 2006 World Cup being held in Germany makes it likely that a European team may emerge victorious this time around.

X X-rated

It's not only nasty tackles that should come with a health warning. Sometimes, the things these footballers get up to off the pitch...!

Y Yellow card

Handed out more readily than confetti at a wedding, you need only sneeze these days and the ref will give you a caution.

Z Zzzzzzz

We all like to moan about it, but how dull would life be without football? Answer? VERY!!

GAME FOR A LAUGH

A DIFFERENT LOOK AT THE CRAZY WORLD OF FOOTBALL

Carlisle realised they would have to stop drinking Dr. Jekyll's half-time potion.

Wish I'd listened to the boss and gone to the loo before we came out of the tunnel.

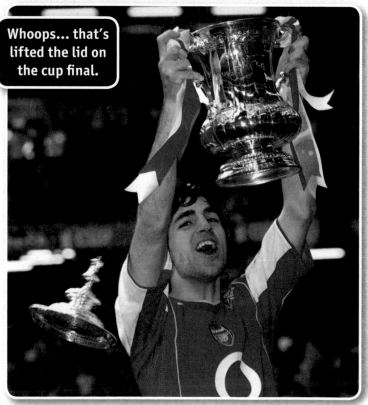

Whoops... that's lifted the lid on the cup final.

Come on ref, have a word! That's a bum decision....

18

Ken Bates finally managed to sneak back into Stamford Bridge.

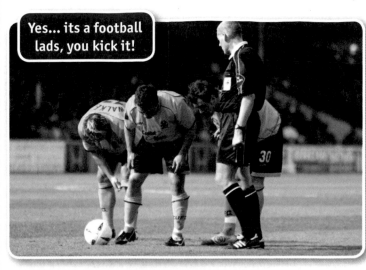

Yes... its a football lads, you kick it!

Who said those nutty Liverpool fans were out of their tree?

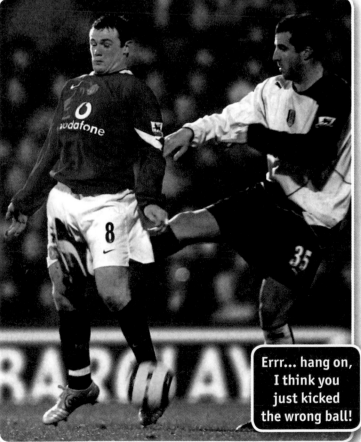

Errr... hang on, I think you just kicked the wrong ball!

The boss said make sure we sit on the ball for the last few minutes, so I did.

BATTLE OF THE EURO STARS

Liverpool or Man United? They both won the UEFA Champions League in dramatic circumstances, in 2005 and 1999 respectively. But player for player, which team was the best in Europe?

JERZY DUDEK V PETER SCHMEICHEL

The Poland international, despite conceding three first half goals, was one of the Liverpool heroes with two penalty saves in the shoot-out, not forgetting one of the greatest saves ever from Andrei Shevchenko in extra-time. However, Schmeichel was quite simply, one of the best of all-time, and if ever you needed a goalkeeper to make a save for your life, the great Dane would be the man.
VERDICT: Dudek had a more memorable Champions League final, but this is a no contest.

DUDEK 7 SCHMEICHEL 10

STEVE FINNAN V GARY NEVILLE

The Liverpool full-back was taken off at half-time as Rafa Benitez changed tactics. Clearly not as experienced as his United counterpart, Finnan has often struggled to show the form that got him a move to Anfield in 2003. Gary Neville is Mr Dependable. He suffered a bad patch of form soon after United won their European crown, but has long since come out the other side to show his true class.
VERDICT: Again, this is one-way traffic leading to the No.2 shirt at Old Trafford.

FINNAN 6 NEVILLE 7

JAMIE CARRAGHER V RONNIE JOHNSEN

The dramatic improvement in form of Jamie Carragher over the last two years is a bonus for club and country. Strong on the ground and in the air, he doesn't believe in lost causes and has become a king pin in Liverpool's defence. Norway defender Johnsen had an influential time at Old Trafford but saw his appearances limited due to injury setbacks. On his day he was a class centre-half. The only trouble was, he didn't have enough days.

VERDICT: Carragher wins this one by some distance.

CARRAGHER 8 JOHNSEN 6

SAMI HYYPIA V JAAP STAM

Hyypia has become one of Finland's greatest football exports and still holds down a centre-half berth at Anfield after six years at the club. He reads the game well and also has the knack of joining the attack and scoring crucial goals. It is a mystery why Jaap Stam is still not at Old Trafford. A fall out with Sir Alex Ferguson saw one of United's best defenders whisked away and transferred to AC Milan in Italy. On the losing side against Liverpool in last season's final.

VERDICT: The flying Finn or the Dutch master? A close call.

HYYPIA 7 STAM 8

DJIMI TRAORE V DENIS IRWIN

You never know quite what you're going to get with the gangly Frenchman. When Traore is good he looks very good, when he's bad, he is awful. However, he can run all day and does possess a neat touch. It would be difficult to name a more consistent full-back ever in English football than Denis Irwin. Not as adventurous coming forward as Traore, although he was no stranger to finding the net with a penalty or free-kick.

VERDICT: Dependable Denis ahead of jumping Djimi any day.

TRAORE 6 IRWIN 8

VLADIMIR SMICER V JESPER BLOMQVIST

Smicer was a surprise choice to replace Harry Kewell after just 22 minutes of the Champions League final but the results of his introduction were significant. The Czech netted a wonder strike in Istanbul. Blomqvist was also a surprise selection for United's final team in 1999, replacing the suspended Paul Scholes. He never really lived up to the high standards expected at Old Trafford and moved on soon after.

VERDICT: Vlad the impaler eats the Swede for breakfast.

SMICER 6 BLOMQVIST 5

DIDI HAMANN **V** NICKY BUTT

A ball winner and fine passer of the ball, Didi Hamann was instrumental in Liverpool's Champions League victory. Coming on at half-time, he ran the show and transformed the game. An under rated and very intelligent footballer. Nicky Butt played in place of suspended captain Roy Keane when United won the European Cup in 1999. Despite several fine games for United he never featured as a regular first-team player at Old Trafford and moved on last season.

VERDICT: Germany 1 England 0 in this contest.

HAMANN 7 BUTT 6

STEVEN GERRARD **V** DAVID BECKHAM

Shoot-out of the heavyweights. Steven Gerrard has become Mr Liverpool and did more than was asked of him to lead Liverpool to glory in Istanbul. A fine passer, superb striker of the ball and inspirational captain.

David Beckham still remains a hero to so many but there are signs that his star is beginning to fade. Time will be the judge of that. More influential in his United days when wide on the right than the role he craved in the centre of the park.

VERDICT: In the centre for this game, Gerrard shades it.

GERRARD 9 BECKHAM 8

JOHN ARNE RIISE **V** RYAN GIGGS

Norway international Riise has been effective for Liverpool either at left-back or on the left of midfield. Possesses a scorching shot and has good awareness of players around him. A good defender as well.

Whether there has ever been a better sight in football than Ryan Giggs in full flow is a matter of opinion. He still has the ability to take on and beat his opponent and has, without doubt, been one of United's greatest-ever servants.

VERDICT: The Viking comes a cropper to the Welsh dragon.

RIISE 7 GIGGS 9

XABI ALONSO **V** TEDDY SHERINGHAM

Two footballers of the highest talent here. Liverpool fans are only just beginning to see the skills that Xabi Alonso possesses. The complete midfield player and scorer of the equalising goal in the Champions League Final.

In 1999, Sheringham was the catalyst of United's comeback. Emerging from the bench he scored one and set up another during the thrilling finale in Barcelona. Plays more forward than Alonso, but is just as intelligent with his passing.

VERDICT: Nothing between them. Too close to call.

ALONSO 8 SHERINGHAM 8

LUIS GARCIA ANDY COLE

Being able to play either in midfield or attack is a big asset for this Liverpool side and Garcia can fulfil both those roles. Seems to save his best games for European nights and was the scorer of four goals in Liverpool's campaign.
Cole also had a great goal record in Europe but at times couldn't hit a barn door in the Premiership. Was virtually non-existent in United's triumph in 1999, even though he is one of the club's all-time record goal scorers.
VERDICT: Different styles, different roles. Same points.

GARCIA 7 COLE 7

MILAN BAROS DWIGHT YORKE

The Czech striker has struggled during his Anfield career and despite winning the Golden Boot at Euro 2004 he is yet to find any consistency for his club. Full of unselfish running but doesn't score enough goals.
In contrast, Dwight Yorke couldn't stop finding the net throughout his stay at Old Trafford. He formed a formidable partnership with Andy Cole, although both had a poor game when United struck European gold.
VERDICT: It's all Dwight on the night.

BAROS 6 YORKE 7

DJIBRIL CISSE OLE GUNNAR SOLSKJAER

Liverpool fans will feel that the best of Djibril Cisse is still to come. Very pacy, he scored goals by the bucket-load for previous club Auxerre, but has yet to find that form on Merseyside. Struggled when he came on as a sub in Istanbul.
Solskjaer, but for injury, would have played many more times for United. His volley in 1999 secured glory in injury time, and in the immortal words of ITV's Clive Tyldesley, put United's "name on the trophy."
VERDICT: Most bosses would pick Solskjaer in their team.

CISSE 7 SOLSKJAER 8

RAFA BENITEZ SIR ALEX FERGUSON

It took Rafa Benitez just one season to bring the Champions League trophy to Liverpool for the fifth time. It took Alex Ferguson 13 years to deliver Manchester United their second European Cup. However if Rafa wins half or even a quarter of the trophies Fergie has claimed, he will be considered a legend at Anfield.
VERDICT: For now Benitez has to bow to the master.

BENITEZ 8 FERGUSON 9

TOTAL: LIVERPOOL 99 MAN UNITED 106

THE PLAY

ANDY JOHNSON

BORN: Bedford, England, February 10, 1981
HEIGHT: 5ft 9in **POSITION:** Striker

CLUBS: Birmingham, Crystal Palace.
CAR: BMW X5.
FAVE TV PROGRAMME: "*EastEnders.*"
BEST MOMENT IN FOOTBALL? "Coming on for England to make my debut against Holland."
WORST MOMENT? "When I missed the deciding penalty for Birmingham to lose the League Cup Final against Liverpool."
HAS THE BOSS EVER TICKED YOU OFF? "Not as yet - I'm a good lad."
BEST PLAYER FACED: "Thierry Henry."
SUPERSTITIONS? "Loads. One of mine is if I wear a suit and have a good game then I wear it again the next match."
IF YOU WEREN'T A FOOTBALLER? "I'd probably have been a roofer or something like that."
A FAN ASKS FOR YOUR AUTOGRAPH BUT THINKS YOU ARE SOMEBODY ELSE. WHAT DO YOU DO? "I'd just sign it anyway."

TIM CAHILL

BORN: Sydney, Australia, December 6, 1979
HEIGHT: 5ft 10in **POSITION:** Midfielder

CLUBS: Sydney United, Millwall, Everton.
CAR: Range Rover.
FAVE TV PROGRAMME: "*Neighbours.*"
BEST MOMENT IN FOOTBALL? "Scoring the winning goal for Millwall in the 2004 FA Cup semi-final against Sunderland at Old Trafford."
WORST MOMENT? "Getting sent off at Man City for celebrating after scoring a goal."
HAS THE BOSS EVER TICKED YOU OFF? "Loads, all the time."
BOYHOOD IDOL: "Marco Van Basten."
BEST PLAYER FACED: "Peter Beardsley."
SUPERSTITIONS: "I cross myself before every game."
IF YOU WEREN'T A FOOTBALLER? "I'd just be working with my mates and enjoying my family."
A FAN ASKS YOU FOR YOUR AUTOGRAPH BUT THEY THINK YOU ARE SOMEONE ELSE. WHAT DO YOU DO? "Sign Thomas Gravesen's name."

ER FILES!

JAMES BEATTIE

BORN: Lancaster, England, February 27, 1978
HEIGHT: 6ft 1in **POSITION:** Striker

CLUBS: Blackburn Rovers, Southampton, Everton.
CAR: Lamborghini Gallardo and BMW X5.
FAVE TV PROGRAMME: "*Sex in the City.*"
BEST MOMENT IN FOOTBALL? "Playing for Southampton in the FA Cup Final against Arsenal in 2003. Even though we lost it was a great day out and I think everyone enjoyed it."
WORST MOMENT? "Dislocating my ankle against Manchester United when I was playing for Southampton."
HAS THE BOSS EVER TICKED YOU OFF?
"Yes, he's given me about six in my first few months at Everton."
BEST PLAYER FACED: "John Terry or Rio Ferdinand."
SUPERSTITIONS? "None."
IF YOU WEREN'T A FOOTBALLER?
"I'd love to be a doctor or surgeon."
THE REFEREE SENDS OFF ONE OF YOUR TEAM-MATES INSTEAD OF YOU. DO YOU OWN UP? "Yes, I'd try and tell the ref it was me."

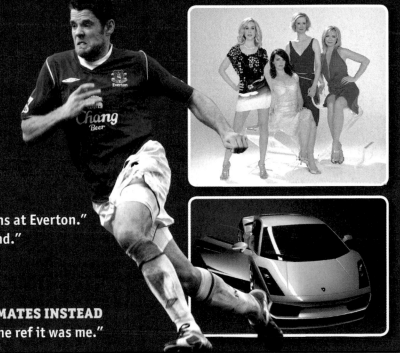

MICHAEL CARRICK

BORN: Wallsend, North Tyneside, July 28, 1981
HEIGHT: 6ft **POSITION:** Midfield

CLUBS: West Ham, Tottenham. **CAR:** BMW X5.
BEST MOMENT IN FOOTBALL? "Making my debut for England against Mexico at Pride Park in 2001 – something I will never forget."
WORST MOMENT? "Suffering relegation with West Ham in 2003. Even though I was injured for the final game against Birmingham, it was even worse having to watch from the stands.
HAS THE BOSS EVER TICKED YOU OFF? "Every day in training. Martin Jol always keeps me on my toes and sets high standards."
BOYHOOD IDOL? "Peter Beardsley, he was such a great player for Newcastle."
BEST PLAYER FACED: Paul Scholes, he is pure class and is so clever in whatever he does."
IF YOU WEREN'T A FOOTBALLER? "Probably a PE teacher or something to do with sport."
IT'S THE FA CUP FINAL AND YOU ARE ON A HAT-TRICK, IT'S THE FINAL MINUTE, THE SCORES ARE LEVEL AND YOUR SIDE GETS A PENALTY. DO YOU GRAB THE BALL FROM THE REGULAR PENALTY TAKER?
"I'd be tempted but no, I am a team player and I'd have to settle for the two goals, so long as we won."

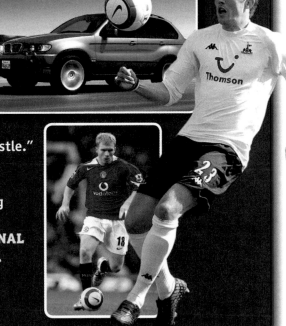

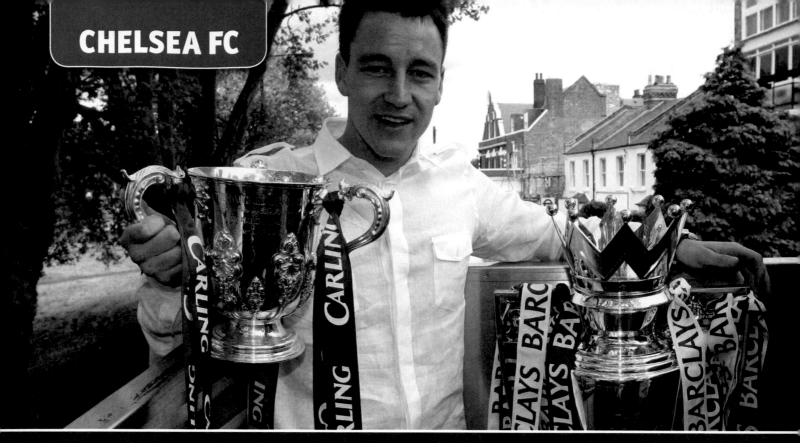

10 THINGS YOU SHOULD KNOW ABOUT...
JOHN TERRY

1 John George Terry was born on December 7, 1980 in Barking, Essex.

2 A product of the Chelsea Academy, John came to the attention of the first-team when he clattered then-manager Gianluca Vialli in training. His team-mates told him that this wasn't the thing to do, but Vialli instead congratulated John on his attitude and ear-marked him for a long Chelsea career.

3 He played for the same Sunday League side, Senrab, as West Ham duo Paul Konchesky and Bobby Zamora.

4 John won the 1998-99 Chelsea Young Player of Year Award. This came after a spell at Nottingham Forest on loan (top right).

5 But it has not all been plain sailing. In 2002, he appeared in court for his involvement in a nightclub brawl but was later cleared of an affray charge. He was also among some Chelsea players to hassle American tourists in a bar in the wake of the September 11 attacks the previous year.

6 His brother Paul (far right) is also a professional footballer and plays for Yeovil Town in League One.

7 John made his England debut in the 2-1 friendly win against Serbia & Montenegro in June 2003 (right).

8 He is the current PFA Player of the Year but says that his club and international team-mate Frank Lampard (right) "deserved to win a lot more than me because he won games on his own."

9 Although John was a huge admirer of former boss Claudio Ranieri, he says that the arrival of Jose Mourinho helped him mature as a player and as a person. "Jose made me captain and that meant a hell of a lot. He works on you as a person and cares about you. I would die for the man."

10 Watch out Petr Cech and Carlo Cudicini. John fancies himself between the posts and often takes on that role in Chelsea training sessions. One club insider says: "John could have made it as a goalie."

ARE YOU FOOTBALL CRAZY?

FIND OUT IF YOU ARE A FOOTIE BRAINBOX WITH OUR GREAT QUIZ!

AROUNDTHEGROUNDS

Which Coca-Cola Championship clubs play their home games at these grounds?

A .Wolves.........................
B .Derby...County................
C .Norwich.......................
D .Hull..city....................
E .Preston.......................
F .Ipswich...town................

GOALMOUTH SCRAMBLE

Unscramble the letters below to find the names of ten Premiership clubs.

1. GLIMDROSHBEUD
2. SHTUMPROOT
3. ACEELSH
4. TRYEATSHCMINCE
5. LIVONASALT
6. HUFMAL
7. GRIMINMYATHBIC
8. DENTINWESTACULE
9. OVERNET
10. SEVURRALBBRONCK

SPOTTHEBALL

Look at the picture and circle which ball you think is in the correct position.

QUICKQUIZ

1. Which two countries are playing pictured right?
2. Which three clubs were promoted last season via the play-offs?
3. What was the score when England last played Scotland in 1999?
4. Name the Premiership manager who used to play for Barnsley, Manchester City and Celtic.
5. Which two countries are missing from the following list of World Cup winners; Brazil, West Germany, England, Argentina, Uruguay?
6. Who knocked Man United out of last season's UEFA Champions League?
7. What colour shirts do you traditionally associate with Stoke City?
8. Which two clubs in England are divided by the River Trent?
9. Name the only club from outside the Premiership to play in an FA Cup Final at the Millennium Stadium.
10. Name the club that both John Collins and Collins John have played for.

SPORTING FANS

A — Bolton
Arsnal
C
Sheffield Eversd ay

Which clubs do the following sports stars support:

A. Amir Khan B. Michael Vaughan
C. Ian Poulter

WHAT'S THE TROPHY

UEFA
Premiership
European champ.

Can you name these three trophies pictured?

A   B   C

NAME THAT YEAR

Name the year in which all of the following happened:
2004
1. Middlesbrough won the Carling Cup.
2. Leeds United were relegated from the Premiership.
3. Gerard Houllier was sacked as Liverpool manager.

TRUEORFALSE

1. Teddy Sheringham played more than 50 times for England. True
2. Wayne Rooney scored England's first goal at Euro 2004. False (Lampard)
3. Jose Mourinho used to be manager of Barcelona. False
4. Brazil are the current holders of the Confederations Cup. True
5. Arsene Wenger was coach of France at the 1992 European Championships. F

Answers on page 111

THE ONES TO WATCH

We reveal the England youngsters expected to make a BIG name for themselves over the next few years!

SCOTT CARSON, Liverpool

BORN: Whitehaven, Cumbria, September 3, 1985
POSITION: Keeper

When England No.1 Nigel Martyn left Leeds United for Everton, Scott became second choice to Paul Robinson. When Robbo in turn joined Tottenham, and took over the international jersey too, Scott became Elland Road's No.1 last summer. But he wasn't there for very long – Liverpool snatched him for £1m during the transfer window in January 2004.

MARTIN CRAINIE, Southampton

Born: Yeovil, Somerset, September 23, 1986
Position: Defender

Impressive skipper of The Saints' FA Cup Youth side last season who is equally as good heading the ball as he is with it at his feet. Won't forget his first-team debut – having scored an own goal during the 4-0 defeat to Chelsea in May 2005.

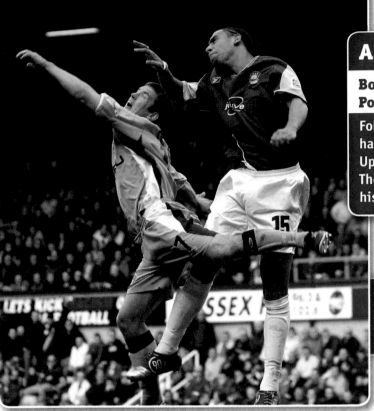

ANTON FERDINAND, West Ham

Born: Peckham, London, February 18, 1985
Position: Defender

Following in brother Rio's footsteps at West Ham, and has earned rave reviews which could also see him leave Upton Park and progress further in the game. Named The Hammers' young player of the season after making his debut on the opening day of season 2003-04.

TOM HUDDLESTONE, Tottenham

Born: Nottingham, December 28, 1986.
Position: Defender-midfield.

Just 16 when he made his Derby debut, Tom went on to appear in 43 League matches for The Rams in 2003-04 and completed 95 outings for County during his two seasons in the first-team. Having played for England Under-17s and 19s, he's now with the Under-21s and joined Spurs during the summer in a deal that could eventually be worth up to £2.5m.

JUSTIN HOYTE, Arsenal

Born: Waltham Forest, London, November 20, 1984
Position: Right-back

Who says Arsenal don't have any good, young English players? Justin made his international debut for England Under-19s when he was just 16 and is now with the Under-21s. A product of the club's youth system. Only a handful of Premiership appearances to his name, but big things are expected of the player.

TONY MCMAHON, Middlesbrough

Born: Bishop Auckland, Co. Durham, March 24, 1986
Position: Right-back

Signed as a 12-year-old after the club saw him score all ten goals in a 10-1 win with his local side, part of a 74-goal haul that season. Now converted to a defender, he was captain of Boro's FA Youth Cup-winning side and made his Premier League debut in October 2004 at Old Trafford. After 20 minutes Ryan Giggs had to swap to the right-wing. Ronaldo didn't get much change out of him either! He had been selected ahead of the experienced Michael Reiziger and Stuart Parnaby by the end of the season.

TOM SOARES, Crystal Palace

Born: Reading, Berkshire, July 10, 1986
Position: Midfield

Versatility is Tom's biggest quality, as this product of Palace's youth academy, can play up front, behind the front two, on the wing, or as an attacking midfielder. He made three substitute appearances during The Eagles' 2003-2004 promotion winning campaign, after making his debut as a 17-year-old. His performances at the end of last term saw him called up into the England Under-21 squad.

JAMES MORRISON, Middlesbrough

Born: Darlington, Co. Durham, May 25, 1986
Position: Midfield

If you want a young up-and-coming player to watch, look no further than James. He's already in the history books for scoring Middlesbrough's first-ever away goal in Europe, against Banik Ostrava, He gives much needed pace in the middle of the park. A member of The Riverside club's FA Youth Cup-winning team of 2004.

LIAM RIDGEWELL, Aston Villa

Born: Bexley, Kent, July 21, 1984
Position: Defender

Liam learnt from one of the very best in Steve Staunton when the former Republic of Ireland defender was at Villa Park. Although primarily a centre-half, he can play anywhere along the back. Liam played at England Under-19 and Under-21 level and also won the FA Youth Cup with Villa.

STEVEN TAYLOR, Newcastle

Born: Greenwich, London, January 23, 1986
Position: Defender

His debut against Bolton in March, 2004, was a nightmare at right-back as his mistake helped Bolton to a 1-0 win. But he's since proved a solid, brave and confident no-nonsense defender, whose best position is central, although he has also played on the left. Came through the club's academy and regarded by fans as one of their own.

MARK NOBLE, West Ham

Born: Canning Town, London, May 8, 1987
Position: Midfield

Former England Under-18 captain Mark, now with the Under-19s, has just been handed a new four-year contract following The Hammers' promotion back to the Premiership. He made his first 16 appearances for the club during that campaign which were enough to convince West Ham that they must hang on to their home-grown talent, who has been at Upton Park since he was just 12.

LIAM ROSENIOR, Fulham

Born: Wandsworth, London, July 9, 1984
Position: Defender

His dad is Torquay boss Leroy Rosenior, the former West Ham star, and Liam had a spell in Devon to get more experience. Fast and a natural ball player who can also play wide midfield, his appearances were restricted at Craven Cottage following a transfer wrangle with former club Bristol City, but is now making up for lost time.

MY DREAM TEAM

Newcastle and England Under-21 forward JAMES MILNER picks his best XI

James Milner was just 18 when he moved from Leeds to Newcastle for a staggering £5m. He was then the youngest goal scorer in Premiership history, having hit the back of the net against Sunderland in December 2002 when he was just 16 years and 357 days old.

Shoot asked the youngster to pick his favourite XI, with no more than one player from any club...

WHO'S IN GOAL?

"Shay Given. We've got great goalkeepers at Newcastle – Shay, Steve Harper and Tony Caig – but he's outstanding. I work with him every day and see some of the saves he makes. Unbelievable!"

AT THE BACK?

"Nesta, Cannavaro and Ayala. You hear their names mentioned all the time, defensive rocks. You can see when they play, how well they read the game. That's why I only need the three of them."

MIDFIELD?

"Cristiano Ronaldo, Frank Lampard, Stevie Gerrard and Ronaldinho. Lampard is so good on the ball and gets so many shots in he's unbelievable. Gerrard's all-round game and ability is just superb. I've not trained with either of them but hopefully that's something to look forward to!"

UP-FRONT?

"Zidane, Adriano and Thierry Henry. Zizou in the hole and Henry right up front, obviously!"

FANCY PLAYING IN THIS SIDE?

"I don't know really, maybe in that formation where Zidane is just in front of the midfield four."

WHO ELSE WOULD YOU HAVE LIKED UP FRONT?

"There's a few. Alan Shearer springs to mind, quite simply because of what he's done in his career, and Patrick Kluivert."

ANY MORE PLAYERS YOU HAVE PLAYED WITH THAT YOU MIGHT HAVE SELECTED?

"Nicky Butt, Woody (Jonathan Woodgate) is a tremendous defender when he is fit. There are loads, far too many to mention them all."

DO YOU LEARN A LOT FROM THE SENIOR PLAYERS?

"Definitely, just training with them, watching them, and how they help you out and tell you things, it's very good."

HAVE YOU LEARNT MUCH FROM YOUR BOSS GRAEME SOUNESS?

"He's great, working with him every day is a real experience. And if you're enjoying training then you're going to be playing good football. Everyone works really hard at this club, which is the main thing."

34

GIVEN

NESTA CANNAVARO AYALA

RONALDO LAMPARD RONALDINHO GERRARD

ADRIANO HENRY ZIDANE

10 THINGS YOU SHOULD KNOW ABOUT...
WAYNE ROONEY

1 Wayne Mark Rooney was born on October 24, 1985, in Croxteth, Liverpool.

2 Wayne was spotted as a nine-year-old playing for a local under-10 side in the Walton and Kirkdale Junior Football League. An Everton scout took him to The Toffees' academy and he came through the ranks.

3 His brothers Graham and John (right) were also on Everton's books but failed to make the grade. His cousin Tommy Rooney, plays for Welsh Champions, TNS, who lost to Liverpool in this season's Champions League qualifiers.

4 He starred for Liverpool Schools Under-11 side and scored 72 goals – breaking the team's scoring record. Robbie Fowler, Steve McManaman and Francis Jeffers had also emerged from this team.

5 Wayne became Everton's youngest goalscorer against Wrexham in the 2002-2003 Worthington Cup while his goal against Arsenal (October 2002) made him the youngest Premiership scorer. His goal against Macedonia in Euro 2004 qualification (above right) also sealed the record for England's youngest scorer.

6 He lives with his childhood sweetheart Coleen and has a tattoo of her name on his arm.

7 His brilliant performances in Portugal – including four goals – saw him named in UEFA's Best Team of Euro 2004.

8 Wayne marked his debut for Manchester United after his £30m move with a hat-trick in the Champions League against Fenerbahce (right).

9 Because of his fiery temper, Wayne sometimes gets in trouble for back-chatting referees. FIFA chief Sepp Blatter (right) said he needed a "clip round the ear" to calm him down!

10 Last season Wayne won the PFA Young Player of the Year Award after scoring 17 goals in his first season at Manchester United.

MANAGER SPEAK

Players often churn out the same, expected end-of match comments. Their bosses are often a lot more forthright and entertaining in what they say....

"It's like being on the Titanic and seeing there is only one lifeboat left and we are all trying to dive into it! I stood there all day with a plastic angel in my pocket. I believe in fate – I'm as silly as a bunch of lights!" **Harry Redknapp was sunk with Southampton despite the lucky charm handed over by his wife.**

"John would be worth a minimum of £50m in the market, although of course he is not for sale. If every ten years we produce a John Terry then the work of the academy is done. It is better to produce quality than numbers." **Jose Mourinho recognises the value of his Chelsea skipper.**

"I said when I left Southampton, the next job I wanted some excitement and this job has that. Even my wife could tell that I was excited. Five years ago if you'd have asked me, I would have said I wasn't ready for it but now I am." Scotsman **Gordon Strachan** goes back over the border to take charge at Celtic.

"El-Hadji is not difficult to manage, apart from when he has these small incidents in his game. At other times, he is a very nice and very outgoing young man. It's just that when it looks like everything is going okay, something happens to him and the fuse blows."
So, apart from the spitting, kicking, red cards, charges of disrepute and misconduct, Diouf's not a bad lad, according to Bolton boss Sam Allardyce.

"When he goes onto the training field the first thing he does is get a ball and batter it over my head into the net. One of these days he will hit me and he will get himself killed."
Sir Alex Ferguson warns Wayne Rooney that he better stay on his game.

"Why can't you let players lift up their shirts? Who is it disrespecting? What's wrong with letting a load of young ladies see a good-looking lad take his shirt off? They'd have to watch other teams, though – because my team is as ugly as hell."
Ian Holloway doesn't think his QPR side would win any beauty contests.

"I've got a Buddha in my pocket - I've had him since January. My son Ben and my daughters Claire and Charlotte went on holiday to Tenerife, brought back a miniature Buddha and told me it would bring us luck. Whether it's had a bearing I do not know, but I didn't have it with me for the Chelsea game where we lost 1-0."
Bryan Robson gets in on the lucky Buddhas act – and it obviously worked as he kept them in the Premiership against all the odds.

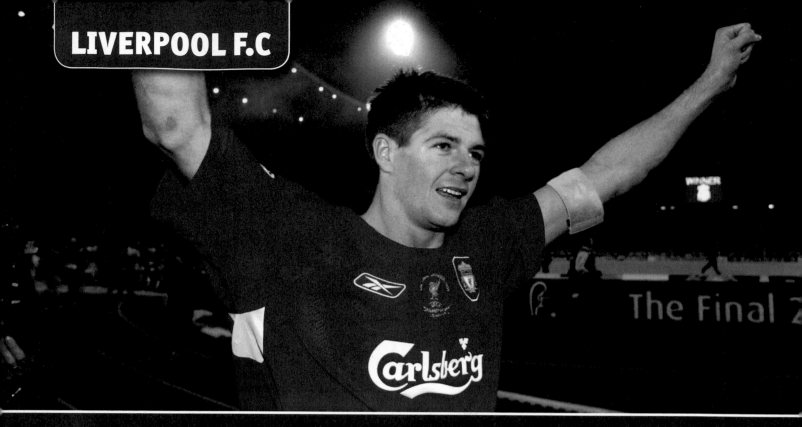

10 THINGS YOU SHOULD KNOW ABOUT...
STEVEN GERRARD

1 Steven George Gerrard was born on May 30, 1980 in Whiston, Liverpool.

2 While attending Cardinal Heenan Catholic High School in West Derby, Liverpool, Steven was so football mad that he was known to go on scouting trips to check out rival school teams.

3 He was the first player from Liverpool's Academy to break into the first-team. Former assistant boss Phil Thompson recalls: "He wasn't the energetic boy you see making those lung-busting runs now. In fact he was actually smaller than Michael Owen!"

4 A life-long Liverpool fan, Steven's earliest Kop memory was the last-minute goal by Arsenal's Michael Thomas in 1991, that robbed The Reds of the title (top right).

5 He signed as a professional in 1998 and made his Liverpool debut in November of that same year as a substitute against Blackburn Rovers.

6 He made his England debut against Ukraine on May 31, 2000 and won the PFA Young Player of the Year award for 2001-2002.

7 Although they played for rival sides, Everton and Liverpool, Stevie G regards Wayne Rooney as one of his closest friends in football (above right).

8 He admits that Roy Keane and Patrick Vieira (right) are the players he admires most. "I would play well for a couple of games and then have an average one," says Steve. "But these two would play brilliantly every game, every season. That was something I aspired to."

9 Man United manager Sir Alex Ferguson is a definite admirer of the Liverpool ace: "He has become the most influential player in England, bar none. Not that Vieira lacks anything, but Gerrard does more."

10 Before he met his current partner Alex Curran, with whom he has a baby girl, Steven used to go out with model and actress Jennifer Ellison (right).

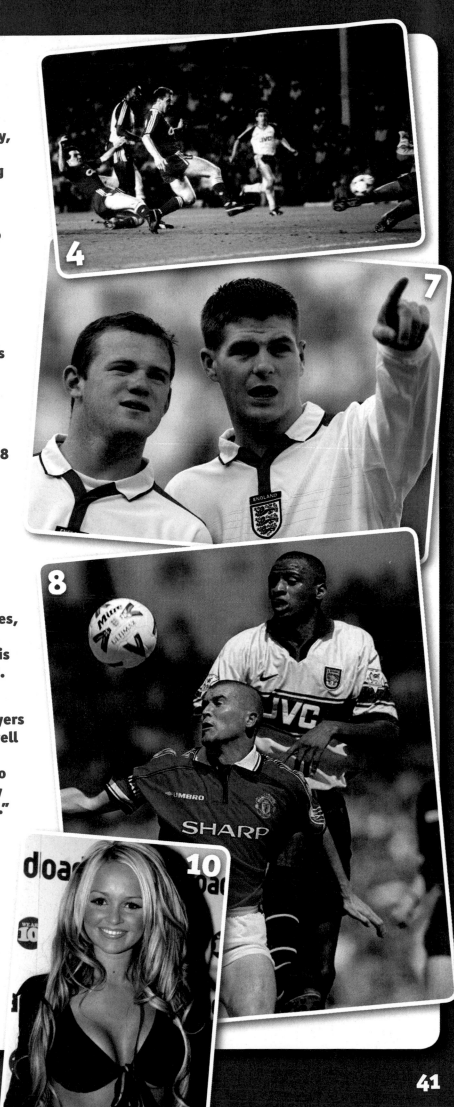

MODEL PROS

WHEN THEY DECIDE TO HANG UP THEIR BOOTS, THERE IS ALWAYS ANOTHER CAREER WAITING IN FRONT OF THE CAMERA LENS!

Thierry Henry – Arsenal's Mr. Va Va Voom doesn't always need a ball at his feet to catch the eye.

Jermain Defoe – Tottenham's striker has already launched his own clothing range and looks a natural posing here.

Rio Ferdinand – Ever the patriot, Rio models the latest Ben Sherman range.

Luis Figo – Portugal legend Figo remains his cool, calm, and collected self on and off the pitch.

Robert Pires – Arsenal's style guru goes for the Alan Partridge look this time.

Cristiano Ronaldo – Man United's winger has an inflated sense of his own worth in this ad for Pepe jeans.

Michael Essien – Ghana's midfield maestro just can't decide what boots to wear this week.

Louis Saha – An unlikely sight at the best of times. Not Louis looking casual, but blue sky in Manchester.

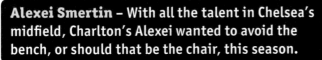

Alexei Smertin – With all the talent in Chelsea's midfield, Charlton's Alexei wanted to avoid the bench, or should that be the chair, this season.

Didier Drogba – The striker will be hoping the Black Cats from Sunderland are as soft as this puma this season.

WEB WATCH

Your guide to some of the more useful on-line football sites

www.4thegame.com

News, info, results from the Premiership, Football League and SPL plus features, a weekly newsletter and a great viral e-mail game called "Stat Attack!" that's just like an online version of Top Trumps...

www.fifaworldcup.yahoo.com

It's not far away now, and the official FIFA World Cup Germany 2006 site has everything you could possibly want to know about next summer's finals, including information on qualifying, stadia and the organisation of this huge global event. Check out the Fun & Games section and the excellent video archive.

www.news.bb.co.uk/sportacademy

Expert coaching and soccer skills advice from the professionals, who show you exactly how it's done. For anyone who's ever wondered "how did he do that?" Look out for Cristiano Ronaldo's "fastfeet"!

www.fanbase.inuk.com

Fanbase is an informative and well made directory of club-focused websites relating to English teams from Arsenal to Yeading, giving fans handy links to every imaginable online resource they could possibly need to follow their favourite clubs.

www.bbc.co.uk/juniorfootball

There's plenty of interaction on the BBC's regionalised junior football sub-sites, including some excellent games and quizzes in the Footy Fun section. Plus, you can find out exactly how to get involved in junior football in your area, if you'd rather play the real thing!

www.thefa.com/womens

As the host nation, the England women's team were disappointed not to make it past the group stages in Euro 2005 but the tournament highlighted how far the women's game has come in recent years – and interest is growing all the time. The FA dedicate a section of their site to the "even more beautiful game" which is well worth a look.

www.uefa.com/fanzine/games

If you like your football fun with something of a European flavour, then go to UEFA's games index, which has all sorts of online amusements to keep you, well, amused! You will have to log in or register to play, but do give it a go...

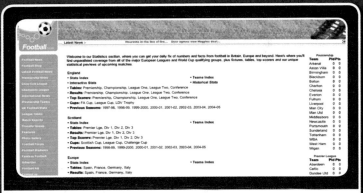

www.stats.football.co.uk

If you're a budding statto, or even if you just have a burning desire to find out who was top of the First Division table in October 1997, then you'll find this is the answer to your prayers! Simple design is combined with easy navigation in this comprehensive and extremely useful font of footie facts!

www.shoot.co.uk & www.worldsoccer.com

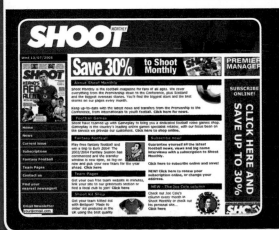

...and don't forget our very own www.shoot.co.uk which provides news, updates on our current editions and access to players' personal sites... to name but a few! For those of you who love their football on a global scale, why not try our sister title, *World Soccer*'s website at www.worldsoccer.com

"YOU CAN QUOTE ME ON THAT!"

"We have to build on what we've done. We don't want to be in this position again next year – I don't think my heart will take it! I know no medals are handed out for staying in the Premiership but success is measured in different ways. This is the greatest achievement of my career."

Veteran striker **Kevin Campbell** must have forgot about his title-winning medal with Arsenal as he celebrated keeping West Brom in the Premiership.

"Our performance levels have not been good enough. Everyone at this club needs to look at themselves and ask whether they are giving 100 per cent. I am not sure all the players can say they are. That is a crime in itself. People are sick of excuses and we're running out of them."

No-nonsense Roy Keane gives it to his team-mates straight between the eyes after a trophy-less season.

"I'd die for the man, on and off the pitch. He is one of the lads really, he's really relaxed in training and all the lads have a great respect for who he is and what he is trying to achieve. We all love him and you can see after the games how he is with the players – hugging and having a laugh – there is a lot more than just a football relationship there." **John Terry** gets all emotional over Chelsea boss Jose Mourinho.

"If I had a choice of trying to stop Jose Reyes or eating a plate of mushy peas, I would take Reyes any time." Blackburn's New Zealand defender **Ryan Nelsen** hasn't quite got the taste for the Lancashire high life.

"People told me not to sign because Everton were going to be relegated but I didn't think so. There are a lot of big team players here and they are all enjoying proving we can prove the critics wrong. In the process, we've beaten some good teams. I think it's fantastic that people keep knocking us and claiming it will never last." **Buy of the season Tim Cahill** celebrates getting into the Champions League after his first season at Everton.

"I know that when I am on the pitch, people expect me to score, but sometimes I think you have to be realistic. The only thing I'm prepared for is that if I don't score or do something great in a big game, I know people will blame me again. But I'm used to that, my dad used to do it to me when I was 11 or 12," **Thierry Henry** obviously got some good parental advice!

TRADING

STUART PEARCE

We thought Man City boss Stuart Pearce was known as "Psycho" for his tackling... but we're re-thinking that after seeing this bad hair day at Coventry!

SIR ALEX FERGUSON

Red has always been the colour for Fergie, even back to his Aberdeen days. Though as Man United boss he needs to keep a closer eye on Rooney and friends.

MARTIN JOL

Who ate all the pies? Would you have recognised the fresh-faced Martin Jol from his West Brom playing days compared to the now-Spurs manager?

PAUL JEWELL

Wigan boss Paul Jewell has seen the hair thin – but that's the only thing that has. He could probably get *Sky Sports* off that "dish" haircut!

48

FACES

IAIN DOWIE

Seems like the West Ham boss has always puckered up for the camera. The hair might have gone, but it's still a face only his mother would want to kiss.

FRANK ARNESEN

Frank Arnesen was very much in demand last summer, but maybe Chelsea would have been less keen if they'd seen this horrid haircut pre-Tottenham!

GORDON STRACHAN

Playing for Scotland obviously took its toll on Gordon Strachan's ginger mop, but it's the gaffer's post-match comments that now take the biscuit.

MICK McCARTHY

The Sunderland manager is known for his straight-talking but shouldn't someone have had a word about that rubbish moustache in his playing days?

SIMPLY THE BEST

The heroes of the Premiership years 1992 – 2005

Most goals in a season 34
Alan Shearer, Blackburn, 1994-95
Andy Cole, Newcastle, 1993-94

Most Premiership appearances 452
Gary Speed, Leeds, Everton, Newcastle
United and Bolton, 1992-present

Most goals in one game 5
Andy Cole (Man United 9
Ipswich Town 0, 1994-95)
Alan Shearer (Newcastle 8 Sheffield
Wednesday 0, 1999-2000)

Most Premiership goals 250
Alan Shearer, Blackburn Rovers
and Newcastle, 1992-present

Most matches in charge 506
Sir Alex Ferguson, Man United, 1986 to present.

Most titles 8
Sir Alex Ferguson, 1993, 1994, 1996, 1997, 1999, 2000, 2001, 2003

Most hat-tricks 11
Alan Shearer, Blackburn 9, Newcastle 2.

Scored in consecutive matches 10
Ruud van Nistelrooy, Man United, last eight matches 2002-03, first two 2004-04.

Most clean sheets 24
Petr Cech, Chelsea, 2004-05.

Most points in a season 95
Chelsea, 2004-05

Biggest attendance 67,989
Man United v Portsmouth, 2004-05

...and the not so good

Least points in a season 19
Sunderland 2002-03

Most defeats in a season 29
Ipswich, 1994-95

Least goals in a season 21
Sunderland 2002-03

Most goals conceded in a season 100
Swindon, 1993-94

Lowest attendance 3,039
Wimbledon v Everton, 1992-93

*All figures up to the end of season 2004-05.

Most consecutive clean sheets 10
Petr Cech, Chelsea, 2004-05.

ARE YOU FOOTBALL CRAZY?

FIND OUT IF YOU ARE A FOOTIE BRAINBOX WITH OUR GREAT QUIZ!

QUICKQUIZ

1. Against which country did Kieran Richardson (left) score twice on his England debut in 2005?
2. Which club play their home games at Portman Road?
3. Which club have won the FA Cup the most number of times?
4. If "The Hatters" were playing "The Blades" which two Championship clubs would be up against each other?
5. In which European country will the World Cup Finals be held next summer?
6. Who was the manager of Everton before David Moyes took over at Goodison Park?
7. Hansa Rostock, Freiburg and Bochum are all clubs in which country?
8. Who were the last British club to play in the UEFA Cup Final?
9. Which one of these former Tottenham players has never been voted Footballer of the Year; Clive Allen, Gary Mabbutt, Gary Lineker or David Ginola?
10. At which club did Alan Shearer begin his professional career?

GIANT CROSSWORD

CLUES ACROSS

1 Country crowned European champions in Portugal last summer (6)

4 See 22 Down

10 Ade, much-travelled striker who moved to Burnley for £600,000 in February (8)

11 Central American country which hosted the World Cup finals of 1970 and 1986 (6)

12 Nickname associated with First Division play-off club, Brentford (4)

13 - - - Parker, Newcastle midfielder unlucky with injuries at Chelsea last term (5)

16 Governing body of European football (1.1.1.1.)

19 Blackburn's tough-tackling ex-Millwall Aussie, - - - Neill (5)

21 National side that plays its home games at Lansdowne Road (7)

22 Nickname by which

2005 Carling Cup semi-finalists, Watford, are known (7)

23 Former Villa keeper, Michael, who wore Wolves No.1 shirt last season (5)

25 - - - Madrid, club side served by Michael Owen and David Beckham (4)

26 Scandinavians such as Jesper Gronkjaer and Claus Jensen (5)

29 - - - Biscan, Croatian who helped steer Liverpool to Istanbul (4)

31 Former Crewe striker, Dean, whose goals could not save Norwich from relegation (6)

32 Steve, son of Ray - ex-Spurs midfielder who moved to Birmingham (8)

33 City that produced the Belgian club champions of 2005 (6)

34 Serbian international, Mateja, who scored for Chelsea in the 2005 Carling Cup final (6)

HIDDENFACES

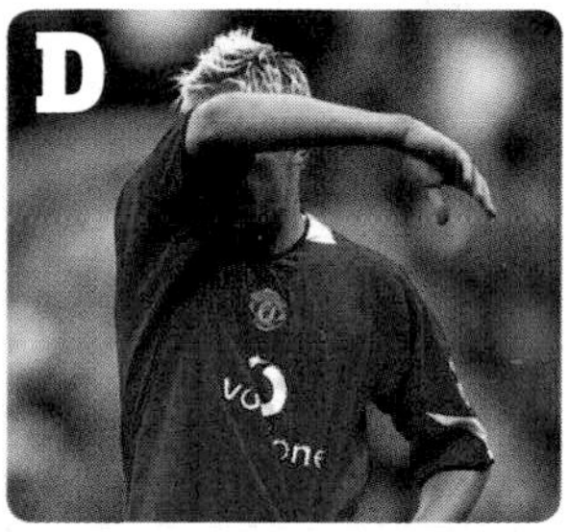

Can you identify these hidden football personalities?

A S. Allardyce

B S. Cambell

C T. Cahill

D A. Smith

WHOSCORED?

DATE: May 25, 2005
VENUE: Match: AC Milan v Liverpool
RESULT: 3-3 (Liverpool won 3-2 on penalties)
Name the goal scorer from the players listed below:

A – Steven Gerrard **B** – Luis Garcia
C – Xabi Alonso **D** – Vladimir Smicer

CLUES DOWN

2 Anfield's Norway midfield star, John Arne (5)
3 Shots that are stabbed up to lob the keeper (5)
5 Jules - - -, the man who lent his name to the World Cup trophy (5)
6 Home ground of the Championship club, Derby County (5,4)
7 Ex-Germany full-back, Markus, who played in England with Liverpool and Blackburn (6)
8 Spurs' Egyptian striker signed from Roma in January (4)
9 Homeland of goalkeeper, Jerzy Dudek (6)
14 Champions of England and the Carling Cup holders (7)
15 Partick - - -, Scottish First Division club from Glasgow (7)
17 Irish defender, John, who helped to get Manchester United to the FA Cup Final (5)
18 White Hart Lane's England striker, Jermain, recruited from The Hammers (5)
20 Jamie, England defender who was Liverpool's player of the year (9)
22 and 4 Across Argentine striker loaned by Chelsea to Milan last season (6,6)
24 York - - -, home ground of League Two Boston United (6)
26 Richard, Ireland defender in new boss Stuart Pearce's Manchester City squad (5)
27 - - - Barmby, ex-England star promoted with Hull (4)
28 Birmingham City boss, - - - Bruce (5)
29 Promotion-winning Italian team - the country's oldest club (5)

Answers on page 111

FAMILY TREES

WATCH OUT IF YOU CRITICISE A FOOTBALLER...
IT MIGHT JUST BE THAT HE HAS A RELATIVE PLAYING ON THE SAME
PITCH! HERE ARE THE PLAYERS WHO HAVE KEPT IT IN THE FAMILY

THE FERDINANDS

Les is the striker still worshipped by fans of QPR, Newcastle and Spurs. His goals and dedication to the cause earnt him respect and an MBE.

Rio, (far right) Man United's £30m England defender, is Les's cousin. Both have had spells with West Ham during their career, another family link.

Anton (right), Rio's younger brother, has also come through the ranks at Upton Park to take over the same central defensive position. Rave reviews earnt during The Hammers' 2004-05 promotion campaign could ensure that he too might move on from East London.

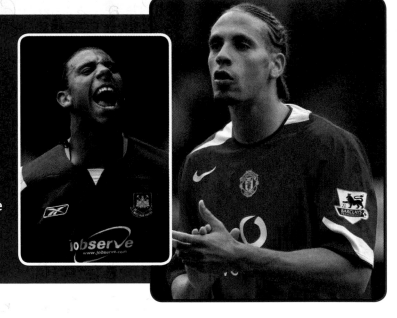

THE REDKNAPPS & LAMPARDS

Frank junior (pictured far left with Jamie Redknapp) is Chelsea and England's midfield dynamo with the ability to score some truly amazing goals. Unlucky to be pipped at the post by John Terry as the 2004 PFA Player of the Season.

Frank senior is his dad, a determined player for West Ham and England who later moved into a coaching role at Upton Park as Harry Redknapp's No.2. (both pictured left). Harry Redknapp played and worked alongside his brother-in-law Frank senior although they went their separate ways when they left West Ham.

Jamie Redknapp, who played under his dad at Bournemouth before moves to Liverpool and Spurs, then rejoined the old man with a transfer to Southampton. Frank junior is his cousin.

THE BRAMBLES

Titus (far left) cost Newcastle United £6m when they managed to prise him away from Ipswich, but the former England Under-21 defender got a touch of the shakes at St. James' Park. The arrival of Graeme Souness as boss appears to have given him a new lease of life and if the confidence returns an international call-up will again be talked about.

Brother Tes (left) is a striker who has plied his trade in the lower leagues at Southend United and Stockport County.

THE TERRYS

John is the youngest but more high profile of the two Terry brothers (right) from the East End of London. Now an England regular JT has been with Chelsea since a youngster, rising through the ranks to take the captain's armband.

Paul, older than John by 20 months, began his football career with Dagenham before a move to Yeovil where he was one of their most consistent players after their arrival in League Two and then during promotion.

THE SCHMEICHELS

Peter needs no introduction as the legendary goalkeeper who Man United have struggled to replace since he left them in 1999. Maybe they should keep an eye on his son Kasper (left), currently in the youth side at neighbours Man City, where Dad ended his career in 2003.

THE NEVILLES

Gary is the older of the two Man United brothers (both pictured far right) and although a noted right-back, has been known to fill in as a central-defender. Has a superb total of 76 England caps.

Phil, Gary's younger brother by two years, can play at the back and midfield, but some pundits believe this has probably held back his career. He's still got 52 England caps.

Neville is their dad and agent. But he's got strong football ties, with an office at Bury where he was a fund-raiser for the club. And just for good measure, sister Tracey (right) is an England netball star.

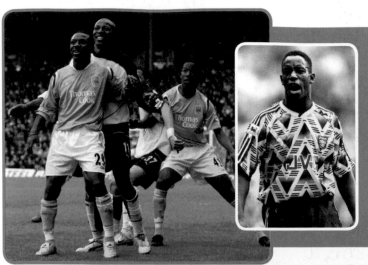

THE WRIGHTS

First, of course, there was Arsenal legend and record goal-scorer Ian Wright (left) who used to terrorise defences. Now there's Shaun Wright-Phillips, his stepson. Whenever Shaun plays in a big game, you will find TV Lottery host Ian in the stands cheering him on.

But watch out too for Bradley Wright-Phillips (pictured far left with Shaun) who, like his older brother, has developed his game at Manchester City. He scored just three minutes into his debut in December 2004.

THE SODJES

Efe (right) is the elder and most memorable of the Sodje brothers with his distinctive bandana, which he wears in honour of his mother. The Nigeria defender, currently with Yeovil, appeared in the 2002 World Cup.

Defender Sam (far right) has, like his two brothers, risen from the Conference, and his performances for Brentford in League One attracted a host of scouts from bigger clubs. Youngest brother Akpo is a striker who, like Efe, last season left Huddersfield. They also have a nephew, Onome, who is a youth player at Charlton.

AND NO RELATION AT ALL

THE SVENSSONS

This is Sweden's equivalent of the British Smith. Ex-Norwich star Matt , Anders (inset left) and Michael (left), former Southampton team-mates, can probably just trace their roots to a distant relative.

THE SHEARERS

The only connection between Newcastle's ex-England striker Big Al and former Coventry City keeper Scott (right) is goals. One scores them, the other tries his best to stop them.

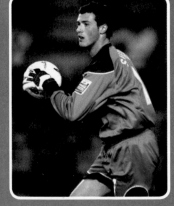

THE KEANES

Roy's from Cork, Robbie (left) is from Dublin. There's a bit of tension between the Republic of Ireland's two biggest cities, but these two will die for the cause when it comes to pulling on the prized green jersey of their country.

AROUND THE CLUBS

Your guide to the great (and not-so-great!) players to grace every League club in England

The Gunners
ARSENAL

1980s...
Tony Adams
(1983-2002)
Scotland striker Charlie Nicholas nearly got the nod here but we had to go for "Big Tone" (left) who spanned all three decades we have covered. With 504 League appearances for The Gunners, which produced 32 goals, the defender from Romford, Essex, made his debut at the age of 17 and pulled off his shirt for the final time 19 years later.

2000s...
Thierry Henry
(1999-present)
Who else but the winger-turned striker, arguably the best front man in the world? Now within sniffing distance of Wrighty's club scoring record after just six amazing seasons at Highbury following an £8m move from Juventus. In 2004, Thierry (left) became the first footballer to win both the Football Writers and PFA Player of the Year awards in consecutive seasons.

1990s...
Ian Wright
(1991-1998)
Wrighty (right) now often fronts TV's Lottery show, but he hit the jackpot for Arsenal following a club record £2.5m move from Palace. He scored a club best 185 goals; earned the Golden Boot in 1992 and 1993; won one FA Cup (1993); League Cup (1993); Premiership (1998). Sadly his England career wasn't so good with just nine goals in 33 games.

ONE TO FORGET...
Gus Caesar
(1985-1990)
Arsenal fans can thank Don Howe for unleashing Tony Adams on the world. They can also blame him for Gus Caesar (right), a striker famed for falling over and missing a sitter which cost the club the 1988 League Cup Final against Luton. A free transfer, a host of clubs in the lower divisions and Scotland followed before he departed to Hong Kong to end his playing days.

**DENNIS BERGKAMP
ARSENAL**

THOMAS SORENSEN
ASTON VILLA & DENMARK

The Villans
ASTON VILLA

1980s...
Dennis Mortimer
(1975-1985)

When you are the skipper who lifted the League trophy (1981) and European Cup (1982) in successive years your place in history is guaranteed. Surprisingly, midfielder Dennis (right) only ever made it to the England Under-23/B team despite 403 games and some 36 goals for The Villans.

1990s...
Paul McGrath
(1989-1996)

Players who leave Man United usually find themselves on a career path that heads down hill at a rapid rate. Republic of Ireland defender Paul McGrath (left) proved an exception to the rule during his 313 games for Villa. The classy central defender cost just £400,000 and his performances earned him PFA Player of the Year in 1992. More importantly he earned respect from the fans for his commanding displays.

2000s...
Lee Hendrie
(1994-present)

A few red cards, front page headlines instead of back and a rocky relationship with former boss John Gregory could easily have spelt disaster for Lee (right). But he did his talking on the pitch with all-action midfielder displays and a few goals. The arrival of David O'Leary appears to have helped, although his England debut in 1998, at the age of 21, now seems a long time ago.

ONE TO FORGET...
Stan Collymore
(1997-2000)

Such talent, such a waste. A star at Forest, not quite so successful at Liverpool, but a record £7m move to his boyhood rivals was expected to inject a new lease of life into the striker. It didn't! Just 34 games and seven goals later Stanley (left) was in another fine mess and was offloaded to Leicester with very little of his transfer fee recovered by The Villans.

The Blues
BIRMINGHAM

1980s...
Frank Worthington
(1979-1982)

The Halifax-born striker played for 11 League clubs, making more than 750 appearances, but just 71 of them were for City, scoring 29 goals. Frank (left) arrived from Bolton for £150,000 and helped them to promotion to the old Division One in his first term. Bought by Jim Smith, he was sold by new boss Ron Saunders as the pair reportedly didn't see eye to eye. A flair player with the knack of making goal scoring look simple.

1990s...
Simon Sturridge
(1988-1993)

Simon (right) played nearly 200 games for the club and scored 38 goals. Cruciate knee ligament injuries kept him out of the game for almost two seasons and eventually forced his retirement. Started life as a YTS with the club which was just a long free-kick from his home. Older brother of Dean, younger brother of Michael.

2000s...
Stan Lazaridis
(1999-present)

A record signing in 1999, the Aussie winger (left) dropped into Division One after Birmingham paid £1.6m to buy him from West Ham. He was in the lower league for three seasons but was part of the squad that played a major role in getting them to the Premiership in 2003. His speed and trickery on the left can often change a game and has proved useful in the top-flight.

ONE TO FORGET...
Dwight Yorke
(2004-2005)

Another player with lots to offer but who failed to produce the goods. Even his own chairman claimed Brum hadn't had their money's worth: "he appeared not to break into a sweat." Dwight (right) cost £250,000 from Blackburn, started four games, came on nine times and scored twice.

**EMILE HESKEY
BIRMINGHAM & ENGLAND**

RYAN NELSEN
BLACKBURN &
NEW ZEALAND

Rovers BLACKBURN

1980s...
Simon Garner
(1978-1992)

Still holder of the club's goal-scoring record with 168 League goals, 194 in total, and voted by Ewood Park fans as their hero of all-time. Simon (right) helped them win the 1987 Full Members Cup, but failed in his biggest dream of playing in the top-flight with Rovers. The fans still sing: "There's Only One Simon Garner!"

1990s...
Colin Hendry
(1987-1989; 1991-1998)

Sold to Man City for £700,000 in 1989 after 102 games at Ewood Park, the Scotland central-defender (left) returned to Rovers in 1991 for the same fee and added a further 234 starts. Vital in their Premiership-winning season. Blackburn sold him to Rangers when the Glasgow club offered £4m for the 51-cap man. Colin won the treble in his first season at Ibrox. Now boss at Blackpool

2000s...
Brad Friedel
(2000-present)

The fans player of the year in 2003 after keeping a staggering 15 clean sheets that term. Recently-retired as United States keeper after collecting 80 caps, Brad (right) was picked up on a free from Liverpool in 2000. He's now played more than 200 games for Blackburn and actually scored an 89th minute equaliser against Charlton in 2004.

ONE TO FORGET...
Barry Ferguson
(2003-2005)

Harsh but true, as he cost a staggering £7.5m and was sold just 18 months later at a £3m loss. A big hit with boyhood heroes Rangers the midfielder (left) discovered that the grass wasn't any greener south of the border. Injury didn't help his cause, and a move back to Glasgow after of a bout of home-sickness proved he should never have left in the first place.

The Wanderers
BOLTON

1980s...
Jimmy Phillips
(1983-1987; 1993-2001)

The locally-born left-back was sold to Glasgow Rangers before moving on to Oxford United and Middlesbrough before returning to Lancashire for £250,000. Jimmy (left) was in the Bolton side that got to the Premiership in 1997. He first appeared for the team as an 18-year-old in 1984 and went on to make 313 League appearances, plus 16 as sub, during his two spells with them, scoring five goals.

2000s...
Kevin Nolan
(2000-present)

Liverpool-born Kevin (left) can play central or right side of midfield and defence but one of his biggest claims to fame is twice scoring the winning goal is against Man United. The England Under-21 player could have chosen the Republic of Ireland as his international side. Has already been linked with a move to his home-town club.

1990s...
John McGinlay
(1991-1997)

The Inverness-born striker (right) was known as "Super John" and scored 38 goals in 92 appearances after a £125,000 move from Millwall. He actually took a pay cut and lost his club car to join them. John helped Wanderers into the Premiership in 1997 with a record points total and he was named centre-forward in the PFA Division One team.

ONE TO FORGET...
Mario Jardel
(2003- 2004)

A not so super Mario! Jardel (right), a former Golden Boot winner, was so unfit and fat after his £400,000 headline-grabbing move from Sporting Lisbon that he was loaned out for four months to Ancona. He made just a few appearances after going missing and on his return to England he was shipped off to Palmeiras in his home country of Brazil. Seven Premiership appearances, all as a sub, meant he wasn't one of Sam Allardyce's better buys, despite three goals in four Carling Cup games.

JAY-JAY OKOCHA
BOLTON & NIGERIA

LUKE YOUNG
CHARLTON & ENGLAND

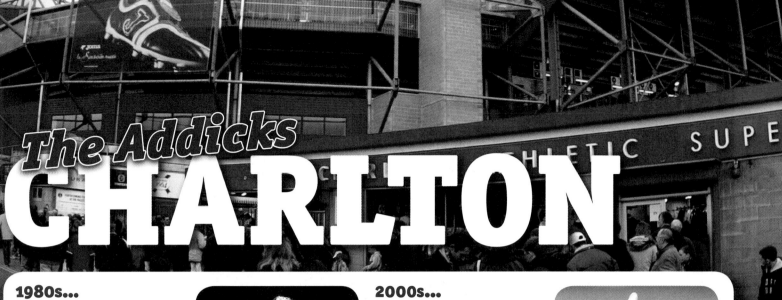

The Addicks
CHARLTON

1980s...
Steve Gritt
(1977-1989)

Steve (right) played 380 games for Charlton and later became joint manager with former team-mate Alan Curbishley (1991-95) – a period notable for the club's return to The Valley. As a player, he was a hard working grafter in midfield. Helped Charlton return to the top-flight in 1986 after a 27-year absence.

1990s...
Gary Nelson
(1991-1996)

Gary (left) started his career as a left-winger but by the time he joined Charlton he had moved to a more central role. He played more than 185 games in five seasons. Eventually finished his career at Torquay before becoming a prominent figure at the PFA and an author of two award-winning books about the life of a journeyman footballer.

2000s...
Dean Kiely
(1999-present)

Linked with moves to a number of bigger clubs, Deano (right) has stayed loyal to The Addicks since his £1m move from Bury. He kept a club record 19 clean sheets in his first season and has maintained consistency ever since in more than 200 games for Charlton. Regularly wins his club's Player of the Year award. Called it a day after earning just eight caps with the Republic of Ireland as current No.1 Shay Given blocked his way to more glory.

ONE TO FORGET...
John Barnes
(February-May 1999)

After leaving Liverpool, England midfielder John Barnes (left) moved to Newcastle where his handful of goals helped them stay up, but he failed to show his true class. In February 1999 he signed on loan for Charlton until the end of the season as they battled to beat the drop, played 12 games, saw them relegated, and by June was boss at Celtic.

The Blues
CHELSEA

1980s...
Kerry Dixon
(1983-1992)

The former Reading striker is what Chelsea still lack: a regular 20-goals-a-season hit-man. Kerry (right) smashed home 193 goals in 420 games and is still the club's second-highest scorer. Earned an England call for the 1986 World Cup but found himself behind Gary Lineker and Peter Beardsley in the pecking order.

1990s...
Gianfranco Zola
(1996-2003)

Not only the best from the 1990s, but possibly one of the best players to ever pull on the famous blue shirt, and certainly near the top of the pile of foreign imports. A skilful striker with that rare ability to get fans on the edge of their seats. Just 5ft 6in tall, Franco (left) cost £4.5m from Parma in 1996. Returned home to Sardinia in 2003, but not before he had been voted by fans as their favourite-ever player at Stamford Bridge.

2000s...
John Terry
(1998-present)

Who would have thought that less than five years ago, after a spell out on loan at Nottingham Forest that JT (right) would become one of Stamford Bridge's greats? Already their first title-winning skipper in 50 years and surely destined to become a much-praised England regular over the next few seasons. A typical old-style, no-nonsense English centre-half with the knack of scoring vital goals.

ONE TO FORGET...
Adrian Mutu
(2003-2004)

Kamikaze striker who could have ruled the world but instead all references to him have been wiped off Chelsea's official website. Sacked by The Blues after he failed a drugs test in 2004, and then banned from football for seven months and fined £20,000. The Romanian (left) was written off just a year after he had cost almost £16m from Parma, despite scoring ten goals in 38 games. Has since returned to the game with Juventus.

FRANK LAMPARD
CHELSEA & ENGLAND

TIM CAHILL
EVERTON & AUSTRALIA

The Toffees
EVERTON

1980s...
Neville Southall
(1981-1997)

He was fat, he was round, but big Nev's goalkeeping was sound. Was the first player to reach 200 Premiership appearances, bringing his total to 750 games for Everton plus 93 caps for Wales. Neville (right) cost just £150,000 from Bury and helped The Toffees to the FA Cup (1984, 1995); the League (1985, 1987); European Cup Winners Cup (1985) and was voted 1985 Football Writers' Player of The Year.

1990s...
Duncan Ferguson
(1994-1998, 2000-present)

Big Dunc (left) is the man to have on your side in a battle. The only person who didn't appear to know that was the burglar who broke into the 6ft 4in Scotland striker's home and came off rather worse for wear! The Everton tattoo on his back, his fantastic ability in the air and skill with the ball on the deck won over the blue half of Liverpool and earned him the captain's armband.

2000s...
David Moyes
(2002-present)

Okay, so he's not a player, but who else has contributed so much to Everton over the past few years? Moyes (right) arrived as a virtually unknown boss from Preston and the pundits reckoned his side were certainties for relegation in season 2004-05. But he took them to fourth in the Premiership and a place in the Champions League. And all that after having to part with midfield general Thomas Gravesen and sell prized asset Wayne Rooney.

ONE TO FORGET...
David Ginola
(February-May 2002)

Even allowing for his disappearances on the pitch, and his reluctance to track back, the French winger (left) had lost the plot by the time he arrived on Merseyside after spells with Newcastle, Spurs and Aston Villa. Made just seven appearances for Everton. Hair today, gone tomorrow for the man with starring roles in shampoo and coffee adverts. Now running a spiritual retreat for celebrities.

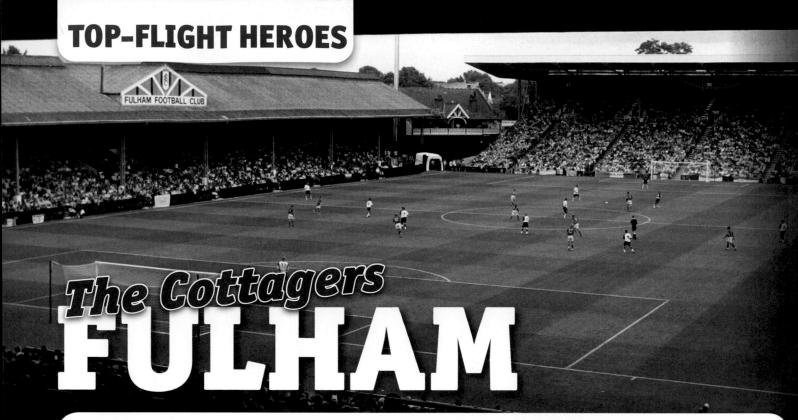

The Cottagers
FULHAM

1980s...
Gordon Davies
(1978-1991)

The Cottager's record League goal scorer with 159, (180 in all competitions). He also won 14 of his 16 Wales caps whilst at Fulham, before a move to Man City. Between 1980 and 1984 Gordon (left) scored more than 20 goals each season, an average of more than one every other game. Scored a hat-trick against rivals Chelsea in 1983, only to see his side lose 5-3.

2000s...
Steed Malbranque
(2001-present)

The £5m paid to Lyon before the start of season 2001-02 was money well-spent for the skilful midfielder with an eye for goal. Born in Belgium, Steed (left) has won caps for France at Under-21 level and is regarded as a vital part of Fulham's future. However, they could find themselves faced with a number of bids to lure him away.

1990s...
Simon Morgan
(1991-2001)

Known as "Mr Fulham," Simon (right) played 518 games for the club and scored 56 goals. The defender-midfielder played a vital part as Fulham enjoyed four promotions in six years, culminating with their arrival in the Premiership. He was then released to join Brighton but stayed with Albion for just 12 months before returning to London. Now runs the club's community schemes after injury ended his career.

ONE TO FORGET...
Steve Marlet
(2001-2005)

The club's £11.5m record buy from Lyon, France striker Steve (right) failed to score in his first seven games and then missed two months with injury. He scored 11 goals in 55 games during his first two seasons, but then a row over payment of his transfer fee was followed by a loan to Marseille for two years. He wasn't handed a squad number at the start of the 2005-06 season and was looking for another club in England or Europe.

COLLINS JOHN
FULHAM

LUIS GARCIA
LIVERPOOL & SPAIN

The Reds
LIVERPOOL

1980s...
Ian Rush
(1980-1987; 1988-1996)

The legendary centre-forward for Wales and Liverpool had just a year's break from his Anfield career for a less than successful time at Juventus. Ian (right) registered a club best 346 goals in 658 games for The Reds, who bought him from Chester City for just £300,000. Added a record 28 goals in 76 games for his country. Six league titles, three FA Cups, five League Cups and two European Cups was a fine return for a superb career.

2000s...
Steven Gerrard
(1998-present)

May 22, 2005 will go down in Stevie G's diary as the night it all went horribly wrong – and then totally right! Three-nil down to AC Milan in the Champions League Final, The Reds appeared dead and buried before one of the greatest-ever comebacks saw them take the trophy in a penalty shoot-out. It was a result the fans hoped would keep their skipper (right) at Anfield, for at least another year. And so it proved.

1990s...
John Barnes
(1987-1997)

John (left) cost Liverpool £900,000 when he moved from Watford in June 1987 and played on the wing, in midfield and up front as he clocked 399 appearances and 106 goals. Skippered the last Anfield side to win the title in 1990 (two years after his first League win), two FA Cups (1989, 1992). Played 78 games for England, scoring 12 goals, but the highlight was his brilliant individual goal against Brazil in 1984. Football writers and PFA Player of the Year in 1988.

ONE TO FORGET...
El-Hadji Diouf
(2002-2005)

Every time he opened his gob someone got wet! Tantrums, red cards, fights with refs, players and even the fans, marred his time at Liverpool despite two goals against Southampton on his debut. Anfield bosses paid £10m for the Lens striker (left) after he'd starred in the 2002 World Cup for Senegal. They let Bolton take him off their hands for a third of that sum.

The Citizens MAN CITY

1980s...
Paul Lake
(1985-1996)

Injuries meant Paul (right) played just 130 games for City. He retired after 14 operations in five years on a cruciate knee injury. Helped the club win the FA Youth Cup against Man United and earned an England Under-21 call but missed out through injury. The midfielder was in Bobby Robson's initial squad for Italia 90. Played in City's first Premiership game, but the following match he sustained the injury that finally wrecked his career.

1990s...
Georgiou Kinkladze
(1995-1998)

After he had spotted the player on TV against Wales, chairman Franny Lee signed the Georgian midfielder who went on to become a firm fans' favourite. Georgi's 120 appearances for the club produced 22 goals but when City plunged to Division Two they couldn't hold on to their crowd-pleaser and Georgi (left) was sold to Ajax for a club record £4.9m.

2000s...
Shaun Wright-Phillips
(1998- 2005)

It's always difficult to make a mark when you are the son of a famous dad, but despite his step-father being Arsenal and England legend Ian Wright, Shaun (below) has done just that. In fact, Wright senior reckons Shaun is an even better player than himself. A tricky midfielder with a bright future – although that is now away from the City of Manchester Stadium.

ONE TO FORGET...
Steve McManaman
(2003-2005)

Macca (above) had the reputation but was past his best when he arrived at Man City. Two European Cups with Real Madrid counted for nothing as just 31 starts, no goals and a series of injuries saw him released at the end of last term.

JOEY BARTON
MAN CITY

**CRISTIANO RONALDO
MAN UTD & PORTUGAL**

Red Devils
MAN UNITED

1980s...
Bryan Robson
(1981-1994)

Blood and guts skipper of club and country (90 England caps, 26 goals), Robbo (right) never flinched a challenge, scored vital goals, and ensured his team-mates turned in an honest 90 minutes. Played in 457 games and scored 97 goals, lifting two Premiership titles, two FA Cups and the European Cup Winners Cup. Remind you of anyone? See below...

1990s...
Roy Keane
(1993-present)

Keano (left) could be entering his final year as a Red Devil and Sir Alex Ferguson now faces the most difficult decision of his career... how do you replace Roy Keane? Answers on a very large postcard to Old Trafford. Hit his 50th goal for the club last term and needs to play 26 games in season 2005-06 to reach the 500 games milestone.

2000s...
Ruud Van Nistelrooy
(2001-present)

The Holland striker's career appeared to be threatened after a serious knee injury in 2000, but Sir Alex watched and waited a year until his target was fit, then handed over £19m to PSV Eindhoven. Ruud (right) had stats of 126 goals in 172 games for United up to the end of season 2004-05, which suggests it was money well spent! Set a new European scoring record for the club with 14 goals in just 11 games.

ONE TO FORGET...
Kleberson
(2003-present)

Oh how a number of clubs must now be smiling and be so grateful that Fergie beat them to the signature of £6m Kleberson (left). Injuries haven't helped the Brazilian World Cup winner, but fans would have expected more than the 30 starts he had made for the club until the end of last term. His Old Trafford days look numbered.

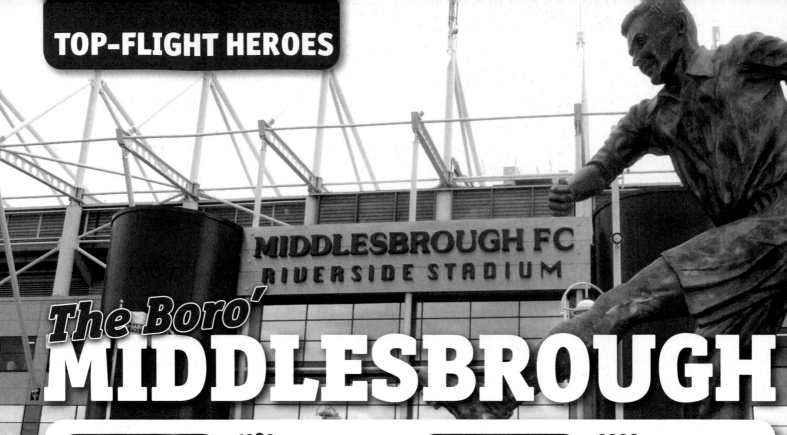

The Boro' MIDDLESBROUGH

1980s...
Tony Mowbray
(1981-1991)

A local lad, a solid central-defender who played 424 times for Boro. Tony (left) scored 29 goals after making his debut against local rivals Newcastle less than a year after joining the club's youth side. His greatest achievement was playing every game as the Teessiders rose from the old Division Three to One. Sold to Celtic for £1m in 1991 and later moved to Ipswich.

1990s...
Juninho
(1995-1997; 1999-2000 (loan from Atletico Madrid); 2002-2004)

Juninho (right) did things with a football that The Riverside faithful had never seen before. But it was the way he took the club to his heart that made him such an idol. The Brazilian midfielder with an eye for goal was a little man who punched well above his weight.

2000s...
Gareth Southgate
(2001-present)

The inspirational skipper (left), took over the captain's armband from Paul Ince in July 2002. He has since proved to be one of manager Steve McClaren's best buys since his £6.5m move from Aston Villa.

ONE TO FORGET...
Christian Karembeu
(2000-2001)

Boro fans are still wondering how this midfielder (right) became a European and World Cup-winner. They reckon the best thing about his move was that the residents of Teesside got to ogle the Frenchman's super model wife Adriana.

STEWART DOWNING
MIDDLESBROUGH & ENGLAND

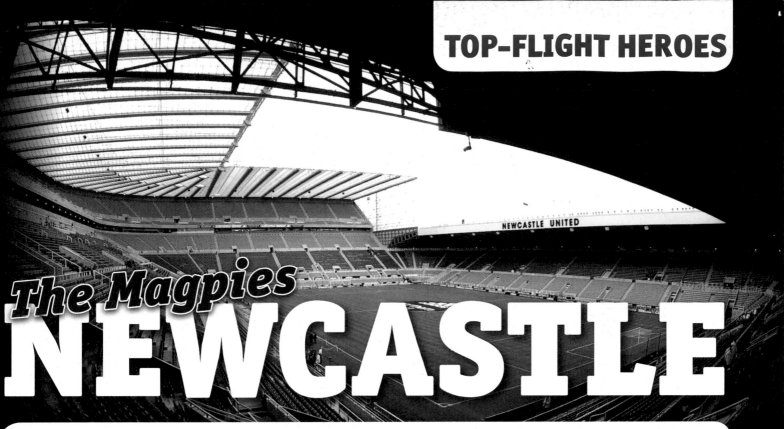

The Magpies NEWCASTLE

1980s...
Kevin Keegan
(1982-1984; manager 1992-1997)

Nicknamed "Special K" by the Geordie fans, he was exactly that on two occasions for the Toon Army. As a player, he spent two seasons at Newcastle, and made 78 appearances, scoring 48 goals and helped them to promotion from the old Second Division in 1984 with Peter Beardsley, Chris Waddle and Terry McDermott before quitting as a player. Kev (right) returned as manager and got them promoted as champions to the Premiership where they finished sixth, third and in two runner-up spots during his reign.

1990s...
Peter Beardsley
(1983-1987; 1993-1997)

Two spells at St. James' Park, sandwiched between successful periods with Liverpool and Everton, made Beardo (left) one of the most respected players ever to turn out in black and white. He covered more grass than the groundsmen as he created goals for others and scored himself with some amazing finishes.

2000s...
Alan Shearer
(1996-present)

He's not nicknamed "Legend" and "God" without good reason. The Premiership's top goal scorer, who is heading for the same record with Newcastle, cost his home town club a world record £15m from Blackburn. A typical old-fashioned English centre-forward with a lethal shot and great heading ability. What Al (right) now lacks in speed he more than makes up for with his ball-holding abilities.

ONE TO FORGET...
Elena Marcelino
(1999-2003)

Ruud Gullit paid £6m for the defender (left) following his exploits with Mallorca in the UEFA Cup. He had to be good, right? Well, it turned out he was good for nothing. The Spaniard was a walking disaster with 19 starts in three and a half years, not helped by a broken finger! He couldn't defend, couldn't pass and the club paid off his contract.

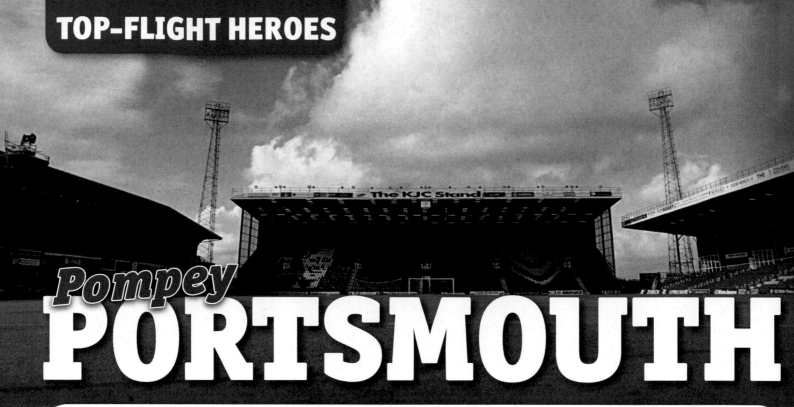

Pompey PORTSMOUTH

1980s...
Mick Quinn
(1986-1989)

The lad from a tough Liverpool council estate reckons he earnt around £750,000 from his football career, but blew the lot before he retired. Scored 54 goals in 121 games for Portsmouth before a big-money move to Newcastle. Mick (right) hit the headlines in 1987 when he was jailed for 21 days after admitting driving whilst disqualified. At the time he was Division Two's leading goalscorer with 21.

1990s...
Alan Knight
(1978-2000)

After making his debut at the age of 16, the keeper (left) went on to play a staggering 683 League games for Pompey before picking up an MBE and finally quitting the game in 2000. Nicknamed "The Legend" he holds the record for most number of games played by a keeper at any one club (801). Played at England Youth and Under-21 level.

2000s...
Arjan De Zeeuw
(2002-present)

Arjan (right) was snatched on a free from Wigan by Harry Redknapp and was one of the key players as Pompey played their way into the Premiership. The Dutch defender had previously played in the top-flight with Barnsley. Voted the fans' Player of the Year during their first season in the Premiership and last term guided the side to safety.

ONE TO FORGET...
Lee Chapman
(1993)

The striker had already played for seven League clubs, including Arsenal, when he arrived at Fratton Park from Leeds United for £250,000 in August 1993. Just over a month later, following seven games and no goals, Lee (left) was on his way to West Ham. Pompey managed to recover their transfer fee for a player who was by then 33-years-old.

LOMANA LUA LUA
PORTSMOUTH & CONGO

**STEPHEN ELLIOTT
SUNDERLAND**

The Black Cats SUNDERLAND

1980s...
Marco Gabbiadini (1987-1991)

Marco (right) was bought from York and sold four years later to Crystal Palace for £1.8m, at a profit of £1.72m. During that time he scored 87 goals in 183 starts and forged his reputation as a lethal and explosive finisher. Injuries meant he didn't play to his full potential during his final season and a half, but fans still hold him in high regard.

1990s...
Kevin Ball (1990-1999)

Two old Division One titles and an FA Cup Final appearance in his 388 games made Bally (left) a legend on Wearside. Boss Peter Reid successfully moved the hard man from central defence to midfield – though a goal-scoring tally of 26 goals would never win any prizes! A reliable performer and a popular captain, he later returned to the club as a coach.

2000s...
Kevin Phillips (1997-2003)

Super Kev (right) blasted 130 goals in 233 starts for The Mackems, set an FA Cup record of ten goals in a season and helped put his side back on the footballing map. From shelf-stacker and part-time footballer, he recovered from rejection by Southampton as a youth and made a name at Watford before Sunderland called. The best bit of business Peter Reid ever did.

ONE TO FORGET...
Thomas Hauser (1988-1992)

The Sunderland faithful reckon the German target man had the heading and dribbling abilities of an elephant. The former FC Basel player even threatened to sue the club at one stage because he alleged they didn't give him the proper treatment for an injury. Left Wearside after 59 games and nine goals for the delights of Cambuur in the lower reaches of the Dutch leagues.

Spurs TOTTENHAM

1980s...
Glenn Hoddle
(1975-1987)

The most naturally gifted footballer of his generation, signed as an apprentice in 1974 and made his debut two years later. Alongside Ossie Ardiles and Ricky Villa, Glenn (right) helped Spurs maintain their reputation as a flair-filled and attractive footballing side. He won 53 England caps, 44 as a Spurs player. He left for Monaco in 1987 after almost 500 games.

1990s...
Gary Mabbutt
(1982-1998)

A model professional, defender Gary (left) played more than 600 games for Tottenham in 16 years despite needing injections to battle against diabetes. Signed from Bristol Rovers for £105,000, he beat a serious face injury and a broken leg to win 16 England caps. Lifted the FA and UEFA cups and earned an MBE.

2000s...
Ledley King
(1998-present)

The tall defender had the unenviable task of replacing Sol Campbell when he defected to Arsenal. Ledley (right) succeeded in that task at club level and is challenging Sol's international place. Has also proved more than useful in midfield and made his mark in the opening game of Euro 2004 against France then had to return home when his partner went into labour. Club captain.

ONE TO FORGET...
Ramon Vega
(1996–1998)

The Swiss defender (left) was a treble winner in Scotland with Celtic but Spurs fans remember him best for goals – at both ends! He had a knack of giving away possession, free-kicks and losing concentration. An average player who scored four times in 33 appearances.

**JERMAIN DEFOE
SPURS & ENGLAND**

The Baggies
WEST BROM

1980s...
Cyrille Regis
(1977-1984)

A trail-blazer for black footballers in this country, the former non-League striker from Hayes was billed as the club's very own "Roy of the Rovers." Cyrille (right) hit 112 goals for Albion in 302 games before moving to Coventry for £250,000 in 1984 where he played a further 300 games and helped them win the FA Cup (1987). Made five appearances for England.

2000s...
Neil Clement
(2000–present)

The former Chelsea left wing-back (right) cost West Brom £100,000 following loan spells at Reading, Preston, Brentford, and at Albion. Very soon after his move from Stamford Bridge he was rated in the £10m class, before the transfer bubble burst. Strong defensively, but able to produce fast breaks and some great crosses. Neil's Dad was the former QPR and England full-back Dave Clement.

1990s...
Bob Taylor
(1992-1998; 2000-2003)

A £300,000 buy from Bristol City, "Super Bob" hit 37 goals during season 1993-94 when The Baggies earned promotion through the play-offs. Moved to Bolton but returned to complete more than 300 games at The Hawthorns in just under ten years. The Durham-born star (left) also helped Albion into the Premiership, but played just six games for them in the top-flight.

ONE TO FORGET...
Fabien de Freitas
(1998-1999)

Dutchman Fabien (left) joined The Baggies from Bolton Wanderers after a loan spell at Osasuna in Spain. The striker lasted one season before being released. Was ridiculed by the Albion faithful, most of whom claimed he was disinterested, couldn't pass, tackle or stand on his feet, let alone score!

The Hammers
WEST HAM

1980s...
Alvin Martin
(1978-1996)

The Liverpool-born centre-half (left) was turned down by Everton and arrived at West Ham after leaving school. Went on to make 586 appearances in claret and blue and achieved the rare distinction of being granted two testimonials by the club. Missed the 1982 World Cup because of injury but played in 1986, although he only totalled 17 England caps. Offered a free transfer in 1991 because of his injuries, he turned down the chance and played a further five years. An FA Cup winner in 1980.

1990s...
Julian Dicks
(1988-1993; 1994-1999)

Julian (right) earned the nickname of The Terminator as a tough-tackling left-back, but he could also make surging runs down the wing and cross with accuracy. He managed 315 games for the Upton Park side, broken by one unhappy season at Liverpool. Forced to hang up his boots due to a persistent knee injury and chased the dream of becoming a professional golfer. But not before there was a 17-player brawl during his testimonial against Athletic Bilbao!

2000s...
Paolo Di Canio
(1999-2003)

The loopy Italian (left) was sold by Sheffield Wednesday for just £1.5m following his ban from football after he pushed over lightweight referee Paul Alcock. Later won a fair play award for kicking the ball out of play instead of scoring when Everton keeper Paul Gerrard lay injured. Amazing skills, great vision and fantastic goals – but temper tantrums would occasionally let him down.

ONE TO FORGET...
Marco Boogers
(1995-1996)

Harry Redknapp signed this striker for £1m after watching him on a video. "He was a good player but a nutter. They didn't show that on the video," said Harry whose man went missing for several weeks before being tracked down to a mobile home in his native Holland. After just two games for The Hammers, Marco (right) was handed a free transfer to Groningen.

BOBBY ZAMORA
WEST HAM

NATHAN ELLINGTON
WIGAN ATHLETIC

The Latics
WIGAN

1980s...
Graham Barrow
(1981-1986; manager 1994-1995)

Graham (right) was a midfielder enforcer who could also chip in with crucial goals. He helped Wigan Athletic to Division Three promotion in 1982 and after registering 212 appearances for The Latics as a player he then returned as manager in 1994-1995. His appointment coincided with an upturn in fortunes and Wigan escaped almost certain relegation back to the Conference.

1990s...
David Lowe
(1982-1987; 1996-1999)

David's spectacular overhead kick helped Wigan win the Freight Rover Trophy in 1985. He moved on to Ipswich and then Leicester before returning for a second spell during which he became The Latics all-time League goalscorer in 1998 with a total of 66. David (left) also helped them lift the Division Three title in 1997. Played with current boss Paul Jewell for Wigan and became a coach at the JJB Stadium in 2002.

2000s...
Andy Liddell
(1998-2004)

Not a prolific scorer as he played wide as well as behind the strikers, but in Paul Jewell's first season as boss, Andy (right) scored 18 times, followed by 16 the next term. He helped them to the Division Two title in 2003 but then lost his place to Jason Roberts and moved to Sheffield United. Scored 70 League goals in just under 250 games for Wigan, setting a new club best and overtaking David Lowe.

ONE TO FORGET...
Lee Ashcroft
(2000-2003)

The former West Brom and England Under-21 striker (left) arrived from Grimsby for £350,000 but after 46 games and just eight goals, Lee was loaned out to Huddersfield and Port Vale. His contract was then terminated by mutual consent. The hitman, whose career moves totalled £1.25m, then went into non-League football with Southport.

BEST AND WORST

We've picked out the best and worst players to wear the shirt for each of this season's Championship clubs during the last 20 years.

BRIGHTON

BEST: STEVE FOSTER (1979–1984, 1992–1996)

Steve Foster's white headband characterised Albion's stay in the top-flight of English football between 1979 and 1983. A solid defender who read the game well Steve (left) earned three England caps whilst playing for The Seagulls.

WORST: JAMIE MORALEE (1998-1999)

A striker signed from Crewe, Jamie's time at Albion was frustrating with just three goals in 31 games.

BURNLEY

BEST: STEVE DAVIS (1991–1995, 1998–2003)

In two spells at the club Steve (right) became a firm fans' favourite at Turf Moor. He was a commanding centre-half who played a major part in The Clarets' revival throughout the 1990s.

WORST: STEVE HARPER (1991 – 1993)

Inconsistent striker from Burnley's less-successful years in the lower levels of the Football League. Steve only managed to notch eight goals in 69 first-team appearances at Turf Moor.

CARDIFF CITY

BEST: ROBERT EARNSHAW (1998–2004)

A quick and exciting striker who made his name with The Bluebirds. After an impressive goal scoring record in the lower divisions Robbie stepped up to the Premiership with a £3m move to West Brom.

WORST: Andy Campbell (2002–present)

The former England Under-21 and Boro striker (left) frustrated fans with his relaxed style.

COVENTRY CITY

BEST: DAVID SPEEDIE (1987–1991)

Hated by opposition fans but loved by the Highfield Road faithful, David (left) was a clever, hard-working forward who scored and created.

WORST: LEE HUGHES (2001–2002)

Signed from West Brom for £5m and told to score the goals to take them back to the Premier League. After one season and 14 goals returned to The Baggies for £2.5m.

CREWE ALEXANDRA

BEST: DAVID PLATT (1985–1988)

The most famous young player to come off the Crewe production line and establish himself at the highest level. Dario Gradi signed Platty after his release from Manchester United and transformed him from a striker to an attacking midfielder. David never looked back and scored 61 goals in 152 games before going on to play for Aston Villa, Bari, Juventus, Sampdoria and Arsenal, gaining 62 England caps.

WORST: JAMIE MORALEE (1996–1998)

Another short spell at a club that was hit by injuries for Jamie (right) who didn't manage to find the target in 16 appearances at Gresty Road.

CRYSTAL PALACE

BEST: IAN WRIGHT (1985–1991)

Wrighty was a prolific striker during his time at Palace notching 117 goals. He formed a prolific partnership with Mark Bright and scored a number of spectacular strikes. A move to a bigger club beckoned and Arsenal bought him for £2.5m in 1991.

WORST: TOMAS BROLIN (January 1998–June 1998)

The former Sweden World Cup star made his name in Italy with Parma but struggled to adapt to the pace of the English game. After a disappointing spell at Leeds, Tomas (below) ended up at Selhurst Park where he made 13 appearances, before being part of an odd managerial partnership at Palace with Italian Atillio Lombardo.

DERBY COUNTY

BEST: IGOR STIMAC (1995–1999)

The Croatian International centre-half (below) played a massive part in Derby getting back into the top-flight during the Jim Smith era. A real hard man, who was great in the air and on the deck, Igor was also a great reader of the game. His involvement was key in Croatia finishing third at the 1998 World Cup.

WORST: MIKKEL BECK (1999–2000)

The Denmark forward joined The Rams following a spell with Middlesbrough. He was meant to score the goals to keep Derby in the Premier League, but low on confidence and form Mikkel never proved his worth to the Pride Park faithful.

HULL CITY

BEST: DEAN WINDASS (1991–1996)

Dean (left) rejoined the club after being released as a youngster and making himself noticed in local amateur football. The hard-working midfielder-striker became a fans' favourite with his all-action and powerful style of play.

WORST: JAMIE FORRESTER (2003–2004)

Prolific at other clubs, Jamie notched eight goals in 34 appearances during his one season with The Tigers.

IPSWICH TOWN

BEST: JOHN WARK (1975–1984, 1988-1995)

During two spells at the East Anglian club the Scotland star became an Ipswich legend. He was at the peak of his powers in the 1980-81 season. John scored an impressive 36 goals from midfield in all competitions including a record-breaking 14 in Ipswich's triumphant UEFA Cup-winning run.

WORST: ALUN ARMSTRONG (2000-2004)

Signed from Boro to provide more of a goal scoring threat Alun (left) couldn't get the goals required to help save Ipswich from relegation in 2002. To be fair, he was blighted by injuries during his time at Portman Road.

LEEDS UNITED

BEST: GORDON STRACHAN (1989–1995)

A £300,000 signing from bitter rivals Manchester United, Gordon arrived at Elland Road with a point to prove after being deemed surplus to requirements by Alex Ferguson. The Scotland man (right) guided Leeds back to the old First Division and helped them claim the league title at Manchester United's expense in season 1991-92. He galvanised a midfield that included Gary McAllister, Gary Speed and David Batty.

WORST: PAUL OKON (2002-2003)

Australia midfielder signed by Terry Venables but never came close to establishing himself. Signed at a time when Leeds needed to trim the wage bill and some top quality players were being sacrificed which didn't help his cause. Paul was a strange acquisition and struggled with injuries and form.

LEICESTER CITY

BEST: GARY LINEKER (1976-1985)

Gary is one of England's greatest-ever strikers, a goal poacher extraordinaire and deadly when it came to taking penalties. In 187 League appearances for Leicester he scored an impressive 95 goals. Gary (right) left The Foxes for Everton in 1985 and went on to play for Spanish giants Barcelona before a return to England with Tottenham.

WORST: JUNIOR LEWIS (2001–2004)

Brought to the club by Peter Taylor whilst The Foxes were still in the Premiership. The manager had previously worked with the player at Gillingham.

LUTON TOWN

BEST: MICK HARFORD (1984–1990, 1991–1992)

Mick (left) had two spells at Kenilworth Road scoring 69 League goals in 168 matches. He was part of The Hatters greatest-ever moment when they defeated Arsenal 3-2 in the Littlewoods Cup Final of 1988.

WORST: ANDREW FOTIADIS (1996–2003)

The striker only scored 18 goals in over 100 matches and frustrated supporters with his seemingly casual approach and constantly flattered to deceive.

MILLWALL

BEST: TEDDY SHERINGHAM (1984–1991)

Teddy came through the youth ranks and went on to form an excellent partnership with Tony Cascarino in the late 1980s as The Lions gained promotion to the top-flight. Signed for Nottingham Forest in 1992 and went on to play for Spurs, Man United and West Ham. Became an England regular in the 1990s and formed a devastating partnership with Alan Shearer. Teddy (left) scored 111 goals in 244 games during his time at Millwall.

WORST: PAUL WILKINSON (1997–1998)

The striker lasted one season at The Den after signing from Barnsley. Scored three goals in 30 appearances before going to Northampton Town.

NORWICH CITY

BEST: BRYAN GUNN (1986-98)

The Scottish goalkeeper was a mainstay for over a decade making 477 appearances for the Carrow Road club. He played a big part in Norwich finishing third in the Premiership's first season and performed heroics the following season during their famous UEFA Cup run.

WORST: DARREN BECKFORD (1991–93)

Darren (right) never recaptured the goal-scoring form that he had shown at Port Vale and only managed eight goals in 38 matches. Sold to Oldham Athletic.

PLYMOUTH ARGYLE

BEST: MICKEY EVANS (1991–1997, 2001–present)

During two spells at the club Evans' unique scruffy goal-getting style benefited The Pilgrims at various levels. His bravery and

ability to hold up the ball led to a move to Southampton whilst they were in the Premiership. Never a prolific goal scorer, Steve (left) will be remembered as more of a Mark Hughes type than an Ian Rush.

WORST: PAUL MCGREGOR (1999–2001)

The former Forest striker famed for his long hair and love for rock and roll never really made the desired impact with 19 goals in 77 games. Many fans look back in anger at his spell with the club.

PRESTON NORTH END

BEST: GRAHAM ALEXANDER (1998–present)

A manager's and fan's dream thanks to his commitment and sheer determination. A very consistent full-back who has made more than 300 League appearances, Graham (left) is solid at the back but a threat going forward, proved by his eight goals in 47 games last term.

WORST: MARK LEONARD (1992–1993)

North End were the seventh club for the forward signed from Rochdale who only managed one goal in 22 first-team appearances at Deepdale. Bolton boss Sam Allardyce was in the same side, but at the back!

QUEENS PARK RANGERS

BEST: LES FERDINAND (1987-1995)

Sir Les developed into a top class centre-forward at Loftus Road. His pace, power and finishing helped QPR finish fifth in 1992-93 when the England striker (left) scored 21 League goals.

WORST: NED ZELIC (1995-1996)

The Australian was brought in from Borussia Dortmund but never settled at Loftus Road and soon returned to Germany after a handful of first-team appearances.

READING

BEST: PHIL PARKINSON (1992-2003)

A loyal servant to The Royals whose passion and passing held their midfield together for over a decade. A fearsome tackler who led by example, Phil (right) was player of the season in 1998 and 1999.

WORST: MASS SARR (1998-2000)

Another foreigner who wasn't quite up to the pace of the English game. The Liberian midfielder began well but was inconsistent and often went missing in games.

SHEFFIELD UNITED

BEST: BRIAN DEANE (1988–1993, 1997–1998)

A big strong striker who was good in the air, but has also proved throughout his career that there was more to his game. Brian (left) helped The Blades battle against relegation in the top-flight and earned three England caps. Scored more than 100 goals in his first spell at the club.

WORST: GUS UHLENBEEK (2000-2002)

The former Fulham and Ipswich man never really settled at Bramall Lane. He often made the starting line up but the Dutchman didn't quite fit in with the style of play and moved on to Walsall.

SHEFFIELD WEDNESDAY

BEST: CHRIS WADDLE (1992-1996)

The lanky Geordie winger was a fans' favourite throughout his time at Hillsborough. With a drop of the shoulder, and a rapid burst of pace, he fooled defenders every time and his crossing and precision with a dead ball made him one of the best players to ever wear the Wednesday shirt.

WORST: WIM JONK (1998–2001)

Signed from PSV Eindhoven for £2.5m the Dutchman had already established himself as an international midfielder. Wim (left) worked hard but never showed his real ability and after his second full season in South Yorkshire The Owls were relegated.

SOUTHAMPTON

BEST: MATT LE TISSIER (1986-2002)

Without question the best player ever to play for The Saints. Le Tiss (below) is one of the most naturally gifted English players to have graced the Premiership. He scored the goals that kept Southampton in the top league season-after-season and did it with style. Known as "Le God" by the St. Mary's faithful.

WORST: ALI DIA (1996)

Boss Graeme Souness signed Dia believing he was the cousin of the great George Weah after the player's agent impersonated Weah on the phone. This tale was as accurate as Dia's finishing and the striker left the club within weeks having played one game in which he came on as a sub and was later substituted.

STOKE CITY

BEST: MARK STEIN (1991-1993)

Mark formed a deadly partnership with Wayne Biggins as the club won the Division Two title. A quick, lively striker with an eye for goal Mark is still held in high regard in the Potteries for his 56 goals in two seasons. Later returned to the club on loan after a spell in the Premier League with Chelsea.

WORST: KYLE LIGHTBOURNE (1997-2001)

One of Chris Kamara's first signings as Stoke boss, Bermuda striker Kyle (left) struggled to make an impact and the goals never flowed. He scored 21 times in more than 100 first-team appearances after a £500,000 move from Walsall.

WATFORD

BEST: LUTHER BLISSETT (1976-1992)

Luther (right) holds The Hornets' all-time appearances and highest goal-scorer records. During his time at Vicarage Road Luther became the first black player to score for England.

WORST: RAMON VEGA (2001-2002)

The former Spurs and Switzerland defender was one of the players brought in during Gianluca Vialli's disastrous spell in charge at Watford. He struggled to adapt to the different style of play, couldn't justify his high wages and soon moved to France.

WOLVES

BEST: STEVE BULL (1986-1999)

Bully (left) became a Molineux legend after scoring 306 goals in 504 appearances. His exploits helped him gain international recognition despite never playing in the top-flight. Steve was a member of England's Italia '90 World Cup squad.

WORST: CEDERIC ROUSSEL (2000-2002)

The young Belgian striker never recaptured the form he had shown at Coventry City. After a spell blighted by injuries Cederic only managed to score twice and returned home to Belgium.

LEAGUE 1'S FINEST PLAYERS

It was originally Division Three, then it became Division Two. Now it's known as League One... and here's the pick of the best players to represent the teams in England's third tier

BARNSLEY
CLINT MARCELLE

The Trinidad and Tobago international brought some glamour and excitement to Oakwell and played a massive part in their Premiership promotion push. Clint scored some great goals and orchestrated the way The Tykes played.

BLACKPOOL
DAVE BAMBER

During his two spells at Bloomfield Road (1979–83 and 1990–95) the tall striker scored many important goals for The Seasiders.

BOURNEMOUTH
MATT HOLLAND

Signed from West Ham in 1995 Matt Holland went on to become one of The Cherries' most consistent midfielders. Strong in the tackle, good on the ball and with an eye for a goal he brought stability to the club when their financial state was uncertain. Moved to Ipswich Town where he enhanced his reputation and gained recognition with the Republic of Ireland.

BRADFORD CITY

STUART MCCALL

A true hero to all Bradford City fans, not only for his exploits on the pitch but also for the work he did with those affected by the fire at Valley Parade in 1985. Stuart was instrumental in Bradford's promotion to the Premier League in 1999 and supporters will never forget his battling midfield qualities.

BRENTFORD
DEAN HOLDSWORTH

Deano was a prolific scorer for The Bees and established himself as one of the best strikers outside of the Premier League until London rivals Wimbledon snapped him up.

BRISTOL CITY
DARIUSZ DZIEKANOWSKI

The Polish international was one of the most technically gifted players to ever represent The Robins. He gained 62 Poland caps and was idolised by City fans.

CHESTERFIELD

KEVIN DAVIES

Made his name as a raw young striker at Saltergate and played an important part in Chesterfield's famous FA Cup run in 1998 when they reached the semi-finals and cruelly lost to Middlesbrough.

COLCHESTER UNITED
MARK KINSELLA

Clever and hard-working central midfielder who gave great service to Colchester. Mark went on to become just as influential at Charlton Athletic who he helped to establish in the big league, and became a full Republic of Ireland international.

DONCASTER ROVERS
MICHAEL MCINDOE

A tricky, flying winger whose flashy white boots made him stand out just as much as his skills. Signed from Yeovil Town, Michael played an important part in Doncaster's Division Three victory providing many inch-perfect crosses for his team-mates.

GILLINGHAM

ROBERT TAYLOR

The typical traditional English centre-forward, Robert was signed from Brentford, and after a slow start became a vital goalscorer for The Gills.

HARTLEPOOL UNITED

JOE ALLON

Geordie Joe had two spells at Hartlepool (1988–91 and 1995–98) and was one of the club's greatest-ever strikers. He stands sixth in the all-time scorers' list for Pools' and was top scorer in three of his seasons at the Victoria Ground.

HUDDERSFIELD TOWN
ANDY BOOTH

Big, strong centre-forward who had two spells with The Terriers either side of a stint with Sheffield Wednesday. Andy made his name at Huddersfield as a striker good in the air and on the deck.

MK DONS
ALAN CORK

From the days when The Dons were known as Wimbledon, Corky is the club's record scorer in the Football League with 149 in 413 games. Was part of the famous 1988 FA Cup-winning side.

PORT VALE
ROBBIE EARLE

Possibly one of the most underrated players to have played in the Premier League since its inception. A goal-scoring midfielder, Robbie made his name in the lower divisions with Port Vale.

NOTTINGHAM FOREST

STUART PEARCE

Quite simply one of the best English defenders of all-time. Psycho was an ultra-competitive take-no-prisoners left-back who was a hero for club and country throughout the 1980s and 1990s. Now Man City boss, he was also noted for his powerful free-kicks.

ROTHERHAM UNITED
SHAUN GOATER

The Bermuda striker signed for The Millers from Man United in 1989 and stayed until 1996. Scored goals for fun in the lower leagues and after a move to Manchester City played a big part in helping them back to the Premiership.

SCUNTHORPE UNITED

ALEX CALVO GARCIA

The Spaniard made a big impression with The Irons' faithful during his time at Glanford Park. An attacking midfielder who scored and created many goals and brought a bit of continental magic to Humberside.

OLDHAM ATHLETIC
ANDY RITCHIE

The former Manchester United forward went on to establish himself as a Latics legend. Signed in 1987 from Leeds, a powerful striker who was classy and composed on the ball.

SOUTHEND UNITED

CHRIS POWELL

Reliable and hard working left-back who has constantly improved and raised his game throughout his career. Played a major part in The Shrimpers most successful period in the early 1990s. Won England recognition at Charlton Athletic.

SWANSEA CITY

ROGER FREESTONE

Signed from Chelsea in 1991, keeper Roger went on to provide more than a decade of service, making over 600 first-team appearances in all competitions and also turned out for Wales.

SWINDON TOWN

STEVE WHITE

Joined the club in 1986 from Bristol Rovers, a striker who regularly made double-figures in the goal scoring charts. His best campaign was 1989-90 when he hit 29.

TRANMERE ROVERS

JOHN ALDRIDGE

One of the greatest goalscorers to grace the English game, the former Liverpool striker moved to Tranmere in 1991 after a successful spell in Spain with Real Sociedad. Scored 40 goals during his first season at Prenton Park and became player-boss five years later. Hung up his boots in 1998 after a career total of 882 appearances and 474 goals which made him British football's record goal scorer.

WALSALL

JIMMY WALKER

A very good young keeper who performed heroics between the sticks for The Saddlers with 476 first-team appearances. One of the smallest keepers in the league at 5ft 11in but a brave and brilliant shot-stopper. Played a major part in two promotion-winning sides.

YEOVIL TOWN

WARREN PATMORE

Scored 140 goals in 287 first-team appearances for The Glovers during 1995 and 2001. A typical big, strong striker who remained a fans' favourite despite moving to rivals Rushden and Diamonds.

LEAGUE 2'S ALL-STARS

Division Four, Division Three, now known as League Two, it's always been regarded as the final rung on league football's ladder. Here are the greatest players to turn out for its current teams during the last 20 years.

BARNET: GARY BULL

Brother of Wolves' legend Steve and also a prolific goal-getter in his own right. His goal scoring exploits played a big part in Barnet's promotion into the Football League in the early 1990s. Hit 46 goals in 106 appearances.

BOSTON UNITED: PAUL BASTOCK

The highly regarded keeper holds the all-time appearance record for The Pilgrims. He joined the club in 1992 when they were lower than Conference level and helped them back into the League during his 12-year stint at York Street.

BRISTOL ROVERS: IAN HOLLOWAY

Hard-working midfielder who always gave 110 per cent. A Rovers fan through and through and wore his heart on his sleeve as a player and manger of the West Country club. Now boss at QPR.

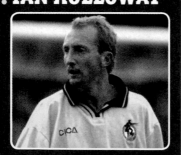

BURY: CRAIG MADDEN

Prolific goal scorer for The Shakers who managed 35 goals in one season. A loyal servant at Gigg Lane.

CARLISLE UNITED: DAVID REEVES

Big, strong centre-forward signed from Notts County in 1993 who became a regular scorer and cult hero for The Cumbrians.

CHELTENHAM TOWN: NEIL GRAYSON

Moved to Whaddon Road in 1998 when boss Steve Cotterill signed him as a 33-year-old. A determined and strong striker he inspired The Robins to reach the Football League in 1999.

CHESTER CITY: GARY BENNETT

Hard working and brave striker who was a regular goal scorer during three spells with the club. His combative approach earned him the nickname "Psycho" from the Deva Stadium faithful.

DARLINGTON: CRAIG LIDDLE

One of the best defenders to play for The Quakers, Liddle was strong in the tackle, committed and good in the air. He made more than 300 appearances in all competitions during a seven-year spell.

GRIMSBY TOWN: CLIVE MENDONCA

Classy striker who scored for fun in the lower leagues and could well have established himself as a Premier League goal scorer at Charlton if not for injury problems. His most successful period was at Grimsby.

LEYTON ORIENT: CARL GRIFFITHS

A striker with a great lower league goal-scoring record, Carl regularly notched for the Brisbane Road club.

LINCOLN CITY: GARETH AINSWORTH

Direct goal scoring winger who made his name at Sincil Bank during the John Beck era. In his three seasons at the club Gareth created and scored many Imps' goals before Port Vale snapped him up in 1998.

MACCLESFIELD TOWN: JOHN ASKEY

Loyal servant to the Moss Rose club who made over 700 appearances across four divisions. Helped the club into the Football League and to promotion to Division Two under Sammy McIlroy in 1996-97 and 1997-98.

MANSFIELD TOWN: PHIL STANT

A Stags' legend who was a prolific scorer during the two seasons he was at Field Mill, scoring many of his goals with his head.

NORTHAMPTON TOWN: IAN SAMPSON

A no-nonsense central-defender who made 449 senior appearances for The Cobblers, helping the side to two promotions during his lengthy career.

NOTTS COUNTY: TOMMY JOHNSON

His goals were a major factor in The Magpies reaching the top-flight in 1991. The Geordie striker used his pace and predatory instincts to tear defences apart.

OXFORD UNITED: JOHN ALDRIDGE

The second time Aldo's name is mentioned in our listings, and it's no surprise! Made his name as a young striker at Oxford United scoring an impressive 90 goals in just 141 appearances. The Republic of Ireland star signed for Liverpool for £775,000 in 1987.

PETERBOROUGH UNITED: KEN CHARLERY

During three different spells with Posh, Ken was a regular goal scorer who worked tirelessly for the cause.

SHREWSBURY TOWN: DEAN SPINK

Signed from Aston Villa, ever-versatile Dean could play either as a centre-half or striker. He went on to make over 300 appearances for The Shrews over an eight-year period at Gay Meadow.

ROCHDALE UNITED: ALAN REEVES

One of the greatest defenders to have played at Spotland. Either at right-back or as a centre-half Alan held The Dale defence together before a move to the Premier League with Wimbledon in 1994.

RUSHDEN AND DIAMONDS: PAUL UNDERWOOD

Former club captain and an exceptionally consistent performer. The left-sided defender made more than 200 appearances for the Nene Park club and led them to the 2002-03 Third Division title.

STOCKPORT COUNTY: KEVIN FRANCIS

The 6ft 7in striker stood out on the pitch because of his height but also had an impressive scoring record for County with 88 League goals in just 156 appearances. Formed an impressive partnership with Andy Preece.

TORQUAY UNITED: RODNEY JACK

The St. Vincent striker made his name at Plainmoor with his pace and great finishing ability. Moved to Crewe Alexandra for £500,000 in 1998.

WREXHAM: GARY BENNETT

Signed from bitter rivals Chester City, Gary's goals soon convinced the Racecourse Ground faithful he was a top quality striker during two spells at the club.

WYCOMBE WANDERERS: DAVE CARROLL

Dave played for The Chairboys from 1988 to 2002, scoring 100 goals in 602 appearances, including some spectacular strikes from midfield. He helped Wycombe make their way into and up the Football League.